BEYOND MAINTENANCE TO MISSION

Beyond Maintenance to Mission

A Theology of the Congregation

Second Edition

CRAIG L. NESSAN

Fortress Press
Minneapolis

BEYOND MAINTENANCE TO MISSION
A Theology of the Congregation
Second Edition

Cover image: Holly Harris/Getty Images
Cover design: Laurie Ingram
Book design: PerfecType, Nashville, TN

Library of Congress Cataloging-in-Publication Data
Nessan, Craig L.
   Beyond maintenance to mission : a theology of the congregation / Craig L. Nessan. — 2nd ed.
      p. cm.
   Includes bibliographical references and indexes.
   ISBN 978-0-8006-6326-1 (alk. paper)
   1. Mission of the church. I. Title.
   BV601.8.N37 2010
   262'.7—dc22
                                             2009037282

The paper used in this publication meets the minimum requirements of American National Standard for Information Sciences—Permanence of Paper for Printed Library Materials, ANSI Z329.48-1984.
Manufactured in the U.S.A.

CONTENTS

How to Use This Book   vii

Preface   xi

Part One: Orientation

1. Basic Elements of a Theology of the Congregation   1
    Kerygma, Koinōnia, Diakonia   2
    From Identity to Mission and Back Again   6
    Grounded in Liturgy of Word and Sacrament   10
2. First, Listen   15
    Congregational Story   16
    Cultural Story   18
    Biblical Story   23
3. Trinitarian Mission: The Sending of the Son in the Power of the Spirit   29
    Jesus and the Kingdom of God   30
    Living Word of Gospel   33
    From Proclamation to *Paraenesis*   36
4. Worship: Imagining the Kingdom   41
    In the Name of . . .   42
    Eucharistic Drama   45
    "Go in Peace; Serve the Lord"   49

Part Two: Identity

5. Prayer: Your Kingdom Come!   57
    Leading the People of God in Prayer   58
    Let Us Pray For . . .   61
    Lord, Teach Us to Pray!   65

6. Education: Making Disciples   69
      Arcane Discipline   70
      Saints Who Followed   76
      Crossings   78
7. Life in Community: Friends of the Crucified   83
      The Meaning of Christian Friendship   84
      Egalitarian Communion   86
      Pastor and People   89
8. Stewardship: God Owns Everything   97
      Ownership   98
      Tithing: A Check on Idolatry   101
      Caring   104

Part Three: Mission
9. Evangelizing: Speaking the Kingdom   113
      Unprecedented Diversity: Are We Ready to Be Changed?   114
      Evangelizing Defined   117
      Learning to Speak the Faith   121
10. Global Connections: The Church Catholic   127
      Centrifugal Force of the Gospel   128
      Beyond Nationalism   131
      Global Connections in the Congregation   134
11. Ecumenism: That All May Be One   141
      Ecumenism as Apologetics   142
      Toward a Common Table   145
      In Service to God's World   150
12. Social Ministry: Striving for Justice and Peace in All the Earth 155
      Social Service and Social Advocacy   156
      The Critical Mass: Three Priorities   160
      Congregational Praxis   164

Conclusion: "One Long Epiclesis"   169
Name Index   173
Subject Index   175
Scripture Index   177

HOW TO USE THIS BOOK

Beyond Maintenance to Mission: A Theology of the Congregation is designed for use by congregational leaders, pastors, seminarians, and others in church leadership (1) to imagine and reflect theologically on what it is God seeks to accomplish through the institutions we call congregations and (2) to develop effective leadership for the sake of God's mission. I thank God that this book has proven useful to many in these tasks. The revised and expanded edition aims to be even more user-friendly. I offer the following ten suggestions for effective use of this book.

1. The book may be employed by pastors, seminarians, and congregational leaders for their own personal study and reflection. In this case the study guide can stimulate reflection about one's own leadership in the congregation, especially about future direction and strategic planning.

2. The book may be employed in a study group, consisting of pastors and leaders from different congregations, in a process of mutually analyzing existing congregational systems and deliberating preferred future outcomes. Such a multicongregation study

group enriches comparing the strengths and challenges facing diverse congregations in relationship to the model developed in the book. Sharing mutual wisdom can enhance the overall learning.

3. The book may be employed by leaders of a single congregation in reflecting on existing congregational strengths and planning for a more fulsome ministry and mission in relationship to this model. To make such a process as fruitful as possible, each chapter should be read by all members of the leadership team and discussed as a group, beginning with the questions at the end of each chapter.

4. In every case, significant attention should be given to the theology of worship, paying close attention to the question about what God is doing when we gather for worship. One of the most crucial matters contributing to congregational vitality involves the renewal of worship. In comparison to other resources for congregational renewal (for example, *Natural Church Development*), worship is not just one theme among many. Instead, worship is the most important factor contributing to congregational vitality and renewal. As one outcome of this study, congregations are encouraged to assemble a team of people who meet regularly to discuss the place of worship in the life of the congregation and to join in planning what takes place when the congregation gathers for worship. The church year and lectionary provide indispensable direction to this process.

5. Focus initially on congregational strengths. Using the model developed in this book, select the three themes that your congregation does best. Celebrate these themes and thank God for these gifts! How can your congregation next begin to build on these strengths and make connections between them and other lesser-developed aspects of the model? It is important to approach congregational leadership from the perspective of appreciative inquiry and affirming assets.

6. Select one or two areas of the model for intentional improvement in the next season of congregational life. Perhaps you discern,

for example, that stewardship or evangelizing needs particular attention. Dedicate a significant period of time to the strengthening of this aspect of your congregation's life, perhaps a year or more. The model described in this book can be the foundation for a process of congregational development that extends over a series of years. It does not aim at a quick fix.

7. Invite a consultant from your church body, a neighboring congregation, or another denomination to offer outside perspective on your life and mission as a congregation. Ask the consultant to help you claim your strengths and strategize for improving underdeveloped dimensions of congregational life. Such a consultant can be especially useful to congregational leaders launching a visioning process as you begin intentional work on enriching and expanding your mission.

8. Make full use of the study guide in evaluating where you are and where you would like to go. The questions in the study guide cover the full range of issues discussed in the book. Is there a consensus about which themes can have the most significant impact on strengthening your overall identity and mission? Set realistic objectives and establish a manageable timeline. Plan for achieving realizable goals.

9. Explore additional resources and reading materials in areas of particular interest. Each chapter includes a section titled "For Further Reading," which recommends books that can enhance your understanding and planning in a given area.

10. Turn to God in prayer throughout your study. The living God in Christ is ultimately the only one who has the power to revitalize the life of your congregation. Pray to God with the expectancy that your prayers will be heard. Be open to listening for what God says to you as you engage in this process of discovery. God aims to further the divine mission of bringing the kingdom through the participation of your congregation in this work.

PREFACE

Wendell Berry's book title asks this basic but penetrating question: What are people for? By posing this fundamental query, Berry intends to probe the misdirection of farm policy in the United States since World War II. The operating assumption, that there are too many people working in agriculture, has shredded the fabric of rural life.

This book poses an equally basic and penetrating question regarding church life in the United States at the beginning of the twenty-first century: What are congregations for? It may be that we have grown so accustomed to the routine of congregational life that we have stopped asking this question. Relying on conventional and established patterns, we delude ourselves into believing we are providing clear theological vision and faithful leadership. Thereby we succumb to what Karl Hommen describes as "the peril of ordinary days."

Although there may be security in treading familiar roads, the situation in which the church finds itself at the beginning of a new millennium—the reality of post-Christendom—calls for a renewal of vision about how God seeks to engage Christian congregations. When congregational leaders cease struggling with this question—the question about God's purposes for their congregation—a myriad of other distractions arise to divert them from this central concern.

Congregations exist for the sake of mission. This fundamental truth about the purpose of the church is easily set aside in favor of what appear to be more urgent agendas. Chief among these in this age of diminishing resources is the challenge of institutional survival. The "mission" of a congregation may eventually shrink to preoccupation about holding worship services and paying the bills. On other fronts, the vitality of congregational mission is narrowed by exaggerated emphasis on statistical growth, contemporary-style worship, or overly therapeutic models of ministry.

This book is written for congregational leaders, pastors, seminarians, and others in the church as a way of thinking systematically about the nature and purpose of the Christian congregation. It is an exercise in the art of "contextual theology," taking as our primary context the reality of congregational life in North America. While we have much to learn from the varied expressions of church life in other parts of the world (for example, the basic ecclesial communities of Latin America), the shape of the church in North America remains the familiar institution of the local congregation.

The thesis of this book is that Christian congregations are uniquely situated in North American society to serve as "centers for mission," both ministering to the needs of members and carrying forth the gospel beyond themselves to their communities and world. To this end I propose a worship-centered model of congregational life by which to examine how we can respond faithfully to God's calling. In order to maintain our focus on mission, we need to think carefully about what we are doing, both in terms of theology and praxis. This book aims to balance both of these emphases, allowing theology and praxis to inform one another mutually.

The "theology of the congregation" here articulated revolves around two central foci: identity and mission. Neither focus may be omitted without distorting what I believe to be the congregation's divine calling. Under the rubric of identity, we will consider the centrality of prayer, education, life in community, and stewardship in forming a congregation's proper self-understanding. Under the category of mission, attention shifts to evangelizing, global connections, ecumenism, and social ministry. One unique feature about this theological approach (in contrast, for example, to *Natural Church Development*) is the prominence of worship in providing orientation for everything a congregation is and does. The historic elements and structure of Christian liturgy offer the church direction for reestablishing the vitality of congregational life, if only we can afford these ancient rituals the creativity and imagination they deserve.

In this revised and expanded edition, worship is articulated even more clearly as the center of congregational life. The most important element for renewing congregational life involves reimagining what God is seeking to accomplish when the congregation gathers for worship. The chapter on prayer is new to this edition, offering an additional dimension for leaders to consider in deepening congregational life. The chapter on evangelizing has been completely rewritten, based on the insights I gained by working with the team of contributing authors in the project leading to the publication of the book *The Evangelizing Church*. Every chapter of this new edition has been thoroughly revised. The literature references for further reading are completely updated. In addition, the book now contains a study guide with questions for reflection and discussion listed at the end of each chapter.

I want to offer a brief word on the significance of "maintenance" in the life of the congregation. Some have criticized the title of this book for diminishing the importance of maintenance as a necessary ministry task. Maintaining the life of the congregation through the routines of the church year, weekly worship, committee meetings, and pastoral care is in no way disparaged by the author. To the contrary, all the themes pertaining to the focus on "identity" contribute to the healthy maintenance of congregational life. Moreover, good maintenance is itself an expression of a kind of mission, particularly among congregational members. The point of the title is not about neglecting or criticizing the importance of fundamental congregational administration. Instead, the title aims to move congregational leaders to build upon the foundation of a well-maintained congregation into vital missionary outreach. How do we move "beyond" maintenance to mission in accord with the coming of God's kingdom?

I wish to express my deep gratitude to James W. Erdman for serving as dialogue companion, constructive critic, and friend in the development of this project; Norma Cook Everist for partnership in teaching these themes and especially for her commitment to the ministry of all the baptized; Rebecca Bauman for her ready and capable cooperation in a multitude of tasks; LaDonna Ekern and David Frerichs for their help as my student assistants; Judy Schroeder for first proposing Diagram 2 in chapter one; the faculty and staff of Wartburg Theological Seminary for their collegial support and passion for learning that leads to mission; Mary McDermott for her competent and kind assistance as faculty secretary; and the seminary students from whom I learn every day. I wish also to acknowledge my love and appreciation for the members of my family, who serve as my base of support in this and every endeavor: Cathy, Ben, Nate, Sarah, Andrew, Jessica, and Mary Catherine.

This book is dedicated to the saints of Trinity Evangelical Lutheran Church (now Saints United Lutheran Church) in Philadelphia, Pennsylvania, and St. Mark Lutheran Church in Cape Girardeau, Missouri, where I have served as pastor. From these members of Christ's church—militant and triumphant—I have learned the joy of pastoral ministry and the responsibility of clearly articulating a vision of Christian mission.

Chapter One

Basic Elements of a Theology of the Congregation

Everyone has one. Most often it remains invisible until an argument breaks out: "We can't have communion every Sunday." "What will the neighbors say if we start sheltering homeless people in the church basement?" "Let's budget more this year for janitorial service and take the difference out of our benevolence giving." One's theology of the congregation shapes in a million ways how one sets priorities for the work of the church.

Put most basically, one's theology of the congregation is evidenced by how one understands God to be alive, present, and working in everything a congregation chooses to do. What does God have to do with it? Most often one's theology of the congregation remains implicit and therefore unexamined. That is the way we often look at many common institutions we think we already know (for example, marriage). Yet failure to reflect carefully upon the entire scope of ministry can leave a congregation ill equipped to engage in the mission God sets before it.

In this initial chapter we establish the frame of reference for a comprehensive and vital theology of the congregation. Understanding the theology of your congregation can assist you to give insightful leadership.

The theological perspective developed in this book stands in continuity with the early church, exists in a dynamic interplay between the issues of identity and mission, and is grounded in the historic liturgy of Word and Sacrament.

Kerygma, Koinōnia, Diakonia

Three Greek words are frequently cited to characterize the identity of the earliest Christian church and its mission: *kerygma*, *koinōnia*, and *diakonia*. Often these words have been translated into English as proclamation, fellowship, and service, respectively. We will here preserve the Greek originals, with the intention of respecting the nuances of meaning lost in the translation.

The early church lived in acute tension with its surrounding cultures. When one examines accounts of the early Christian witnesses at the time the New Testament books conclude, in the early second century, for example, the letters of Ignatius or Polycarp, one is struck by the immediacy of persecution and martyrdom. Christians lived in an environment that was at best indifferent and that frequently organized acts of hostility against them. The main cause for the troubles faced by Christians was their peculiar confession of the lordship of one Jesus Christ, crucified by the Romans, but for them the source of their own and the world's salvation.

This confession of faith in Jesus Christ might have been excusable were it not for their persistence in seeking to spread these beliefs to others. What is more, the lordship of Jesus over their lives made them suspect to both their Jewish neighbors and to the Roman authorities. A widening breach separated the early Christians from the Jewish communities that birthed them, as the confession of Jesus acted as a monumental stumbling block. This meant that the provisions for Jews under Roman law were insufficient to protect them. Furthermore, Christians who failed to do adequate obeisance to Caesar and demonstrate loyalty as Roman citizens became subject to persecution.

In this adverse climate, Christian believers organized life around three central concerns. The first of these, *kerygma*, refers not just to formal preaching but to proclamation of the Christian gospel in a variety of forms. By *gospel* these Christians meant the message of Jesus crucified and risen from the dead, by which salvation from sin, evil powers, and death had been won. Those who put faith in Jesus and transferred allegiance to him formed a countercultural community, providing mutual edification for each other and proclaiming the message so that others might join their ranks and be saved.

A central occasion for the *kerygma* was the assembly of believers for worship. Those appointed to preside over the Eucharist would also often serve as interpreters of the readings from Holy Scripture. Where there were readings from the Hebrew Bible, emphasis was placed on fulfillment in Christ. Readings from Paul, the Gospels, and other New Testament writings also invited interpretation and explanation. Much of this proclamation took shape as exhortation and advice for persevering faithfully in the face of misunderstanding and opposition. A holy life could serve as a powerful witness to the truth of the Christian *kerygma*.

The *kerygma* was also proclaimed by those doing the work of an evangelist. In addition to the testimony of the Christian faithful to family and neighbors, itinerant evangelists carried the gospel message far and wide. Paul provides a very early model of how the *kerygma* became known throughout and beyond the expanse of the Roman Empire. Entering a city or town, Paul went first to the local synagogue and entered into discussion and even debate about the meaning of the Jewish Bible in light of the coming of Jesus Christ. Where the Christian message was received, Paul established a congregation for the nurture and spreading of the gospel. Where met by opposition, Paul took the gospel to the Gentile population and sought to build a local congregation. In either case, Gentiles were welcomed into the Christian community on the basis of confession of faith in the *kerygma* and baptism in the name of Jesus Christ.

What is difficult for us to recapture is the dynamic power intrinsic to early Christian announcement of the *kerygma*. The living Christ, clothed in human testimony, encountered hearers to set them free from fear and empowered them for a Christlike lifestyle in community with other believers. The message was not abstract ideas about Jesus but rather a conviction and a declaration of his living presence among them. Whether in personal testimony or in the public forum, the *kerygma* embodied the Christ, made him come alive anew in a word event, and re-presented him as a living person with whom one was invited to contend. Forgiveness of sins, deliverance from evil, and eternal life were gifts offered by the living, resurrected Jesus Christ, too good to be true.

The second characteristic of the life of the early church is summarized by the term *koinōnia*. The origin of Christian *koinōnia* comes from the initiative of God in establishing communion with humankind by the power of the Spirit. The undeserved and gracious love of God (*agapē*) entered the world in the incarnation of Jesus Christ to create fellowship both with God and among humankind. Jesus gathered around himself a community of disciples, exemplified by the Twelve. Jesus was renowned and even notorious for the fellowship he initiated—with sinners, tax collectors, lepers, Gentiles, women, and children. Particularly scandalous was Jesus' practice of open table fellowship. The kingdom of God meant for Jesus a community of egalitarian friendship under God's grace.

After Jesus' death and resurrection, *koinōnia* with Jesus continued in the ritual eating and drinking of bread and wine, known as the Eucharist. The Christian faithful continued to gather together, especially on the day of the resurrection (Sunday), to bless and break bread together in the name of Jesus. Through gathering together, hearing the Word, praying, and partaking in the sacraments, Jesus lived among them, bearing gifts of salvation. This *koinōnia* with God in Jesus Christ by the presence of the Spirit abides at the heart of all Christian fellowship.

Given the care of God in Christ for them, the early church lived also in mutual love and care for one another. The Acts of the Apostles reports that, "All who believed were together and had all things in common; they would sell their possessions and goods and distribute the proceeds to all, as any had need" (Acts 2:44-45). Special concern was demonstrated for widows and orphans within the community. The church recognized the value of its community life as a form of witness in demonstrating how Christians love one another. This testimony was seriously challenged when the church was forced to consider the acceptance of Gentiles into its fellowship. Did Gentiles first have to accept elements of the Jewish law and lifestyle before being allowed into Christian fellowship? Not without controversy, this debate was eventually settled by requiring nothing other than confession of faith in Jesus Christ and baptism.

The essence of Christian *koinōnia* involves the quality of a community's life together. Does a community reflect the spirit of mutual love and concern shown by Jesus to those who followed him? Are all made welcome in the name of Jesus? Is the ultimate source of power that of the crucified Christ, and is that power shared in common? Is special effort made to express concern for "the least" of the sisters and brothers? And, when there is failure to live up to the ideal, is there readiness to ask for and grant forgiveness for Christ's sake? Each of these questions addresses aspects of Christian *koinōnia* and is vital for measuring the quality of church life today as in ages past.

The final characteristic of early Christian community is *diakonia*, service. From this root we derive the terms *deacon* and *deaconess*, which designate an office in the church committed to deeds of service to others. The model for all Christian service returns to the example of Jesus, who defined human greatness not with images of wealth or authority but through the image of the servant kneeling down to wash dirty feet. Jesus' ultimate act of service entailed the sacrifice of his very own life on the cross as an expression of God's love, forgiveness, and salvation.

The *diakonia* of the early church was most evident in activities of healing, reconciling, and feeding. The brokenness of human life is nowhere more apparent than where people are sick, estranged, or hungry. The church carried forward Jesus' own ministry of healing by visiting the sick, anointing them with oil, and praying for them. The needs of the grieving, the widows, and the orphans were likewise essential to this healing work. The message of reconciliation was announced wherever conflict threatened to dismember the body of Christ. One thinks particularly of Paul's efforts at reconciliation in his correspondence with the Corinthian congregation. As often as the gospel was preached, the appeal was not only for reconciliation with God but also with one another. Feeding the hungry and needy was practiced by early Christians through programs of collection and distribution. These efforts stood in continuity with Jesus' own feeding miracles and the fourth petition of the Lord's Prayer, in which Jesus taught his disciples, "Give us this day our daily bread." Though early Christian communities were neither situated nor organized to enact structural change in society (especially given their convictions about the imminent Parousia) there was a consistent pattern of selfless service to others that marks Christian *diakonia*.

Taken together, these three characteristics, *kerygma*, *koinōnia*, and *diakonia*, typify Christian community from the very beginning. Each of these ancient ministries finds elaboration in the theology of the congregation here developed.

From Identity to Mission and Back Again

Between the early generations of the Christian church and the present, some changes have taken place. No longer do we readily recognize the meanings of the three Greek terms *kerygma*, *koinōnia*, and *diakonia*. Between our time and theirs looms the monumental shift in Christian consciousness marked by Christianity's becoming the favored religion of the Roman Empire during the fourth century. As baptism became required as a matter of citizenship, the level of individual Christian commitment diminished. When everyone gets baptized, the meaning of baptism gets watered down. Today we employ different operating categories from those of the early church.

Nevertheless, Christ's commission to the church, to make disciples of all nations, remains as valid today as ever before. In order to carry out this mandate, the church must forever attend to two fundamental tasks: *formation of Christian identity and faithfulness to the mission of the gospel*. "Identity" is a modern concept, strongly influenced by psychology. It refers to the foundational self-understanding of an individual. Applied to a group, identity is related to communal self-understanding. The Christian contention is that individual identity finds its genuine expression only through confession of faith in Jesus as Lord as sacramentally enacted in baptism. The group identity of the church is commensurate with this, a community rooted in the way of Jesus Christ.

"Mission," the second task, refers to the purpose for which the church exists. Christian mission derives from the apostolic "sending out" of disciples by Jesus into the world to proclaim the gospel and extend the kingdom. Focus on identity without mission reduces the church to a social club whose only reason to exist is for the comfort and security of its membership. Focus on mission without the nurture of baptismal identity—both personally and communally—begins to disintegrate into hyperactivity without direction. Identity without mission leads to self-absorption. Mission without identity leads to amnesia and exhaustion. Both identity and mission must be related in dynamic interaction.

The model of congregational life outlined in this book is above all centered in worship of the triune God. Worship is the most important thing congregations do! All of a congregation's identity and mission is grounded in what we profess and enact at worship. For this reason, worship is given central place in this theology of the congregation, and all other components center around what we do when we gather to worship.

Taking primary orientation from the practice of worship, all the rest of congregational life needs to be understood as serving its core identity and mission. In this model, those congregational activities that especially serve identity and those that particularly serve mission are each organized into four subcategories. The Christian congregation must attend to its identity by careful reflection on and practice of its (1) prayer life, (2) teaching ministry, (3) life in community, and (4) stewardship. Congregational mission entails conscientious efforts at (1) evangelizing, (2) making global connections, (3) building ecumenical partnerships, and (4) engagement in social ministry. Taken together, these nine components offer a comprehensive approach to congregational ministry. This does not mean every congregation incorporates each of these elements in the same way. But moving from its current position, every congregation will benefit from employing these nine criteria to measure and develop wholeness in its ministry.

The model here proposed should be understood as a dynamic system. At every moment, a congregation needs to ground its life in the worship of the living God. Worship is the center that binds all of congregational reality together. Yet around this center, the other ministries of the congregation relate in dynamic interaction. At one juncture in its life, a congregation may give priority to the focus on Christian identity by building up its efforts in the areas of prayer, education, life in community, and/or stewardship. Particular attention may have to be given to one (or more) of the four component aspects of identity formation. At other times (probably far more frequently), it is the mission of the congregation that requires focused consideration. Special attention will be directed toward a congregation's efforts in evangelizing, global connections, ecumenical relationships, or social ministry. At no time, however, ought the two central foci, identity and mission, be severed from one another. To do so is to jeopardize a congregation's health.

Larger congregations may find it possible, with their larger membership and budgets, to address a greater number of these concerns simultaneously. Small congregations certainly need to operate on a more modest scale but nonetheless can discover ways of enhancing each of the designated components. It is vital that local leaders begin by paying careful attention to its own, existing congregational context with appreciation for the history and resources that are already in place. Some of the greatest tools in this regard are the resources available for appreciative inquiry and asset mapping.

What is exciting about this theology of the congregation is that the starting point for all else is the worship life of the congregation. Even in the most marginalized of congregations, worship serves as a tremendous source for renewal, as the baptized continue to gather together on Sundays. As shall be articulated in the pages that follow, all of the fundamental components of congregational life are grounded in the historic Christian liturgy. We take our direction from the things we say about ourselves and do at worship.

Figure 1 (next page) summarizes the theology of the congregation to be elaborated in the remainder of this book. Again, the various components of the model need to be viewed in dynamic interrelationship one with the other.

This chart demonstrates the various components of the model, centered around worship, with the two central foci of identity and mission. Congregations are challenged to evaluate their priorities by examining their ministries in all nine thematized areas of congregational life.

One limitation of this depiction is that it gives the impression that ministry in each of the nine areas unfolds in a linear sequence. Instead, the model developed in this book seeks to demonstrate a lively interchange among all areas of congregational life, with special emphasis on the catalytic function of worship to revitalize all other aspects of congregational ministry. Another limitation is that the reader may obtain the impression that the focus on congregational identity is something different from the focus on mission. Instead, the focus on identity must be viewed as integral to and serving the larger focus on congregational mission. As a corrective to these limitations, consider Figure 2, which indicates the complexity of relationships among the various components of the model.

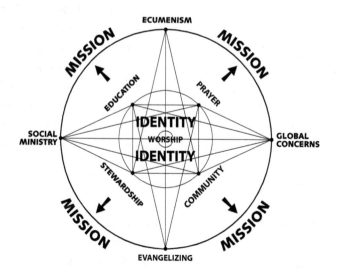

Each and every component exists in vital relationship with all of the others. The necessary focus on a congregation's identity is clearly in service of the larger Christian focus on mission.

Grounded in Liturgy of Word and Sacrament

Frequently one hears appeals for new forms and innovative styles of worship as necessary for church growth and renewal. In recent history, many have argued for alternative liturgies and contemporary worship as "entertainment evangelism." Especially at a time when the church is declining on several fronts, we are tempted to jettison the ballast of ancient liturgy in favor of what appear to be more accessible and attractive forms. This is not to argue against creativity and vitality in ritual. But what distinguishes this book is an approach which advocates forcefully for a fresh understanding of the historic liturgy as the single most important key for renewing congregational life and mission.

Although congregations week after week may assemble for worship using a historic rite (sometimes given renewal by the introduction of a new worship book), too frequently they fail to appreciate the treasure that has been preserved for them through the ages. The historic liturgy (properly known as the Roman rite) traces its origin back to the earliest centuries of Christianity. While there is today a plethora of churches advertising themselves as "Bible" churches, the entirety of the historic liturgy is based on biblical material. Often the texts for worship (for example, in the confession of sins or the hymns of praise) are taken directly from Scripture. Regular use of the lectionary ensures that at least four Bible passages are read each Sunday. Sermons are based on texts from God's Word. The entire communion liturgy is constructed from biblical materials. There is no worship that is more Bible-based than that which follows the historic liturgy!

The shape of the liturgy was developed over a number of centuries. Elements of the liturgy used today were already in place at the time of such Christian witnesses as Justin Martyr (c. 155) and Hippolytus (c. 200). The Roman rite, which contains virtually all the liturgical forms still in use today, was fixed already in the fifth century. When we worship using the historic liturgy, not only are we connected with Christians over the ages, but we are immersed in an encounter with God in Christ that has been effective in preserving and fostering the faith for two thousand years!

At the time of the Reformation, there were those, like Karlstadt and Zwingli, who were convinced that the reform of the church should require the virtual abandonment of the Roman liturgy. Martin Luther, however, took a more careful approach, revising the mass for the sake of a clearer proclamation of the gospel while preserving its essential structure and flow. Among the changes Luther implemented were the recovery of the sermon, introduction of hymns, service in the vernacular, emphasis on the Words of Institution within the communion liturgy, and participation of the people in the entire service, particularly as those who partake of the Holy Communion with Christ in bread and wine. Above all, Luther was concerned to reform the idea of the mass as a sacrifice offered to God by the priest and replace it with belief in a gracious God who meets us in Christ through the sacrament as the center of worship.

Where liturgy remains vibrant, this conviction always prevails: God is the primary actor in worship! This means that worship itself is sacramental in character; Christ himself is alive and meets us in Word and Sacrament, and we are transformed. A congregation that places its trust in God's gracious presence in worship, Word and Sacrament, is establishing the foundation upon which the entirety of its ministry can develop and thrive. A congregation that underestimates the power of God in worship is in danger of losing not only its zeal for mission but its very soul.

An interpretation of worship is the thread that ties together this entire book. While there are numerous angles from which one can explore what happens in worship, for theological purposes it is vital that we educate the church about what it is *God is doing* in and through us when we participate in worship. This does not mean we turn the worship service into a lecture hall or Bible discussion group. Rather, one's very participation in the historic liturgy is an immersion in Christian reality that we need to articulate and reflect upon more intentionally in order to understand what is happening to us when we worship. Proper appreciation for the drama of worship provides the theological basis for everything a congregation does in education, stewardship, evangelism, social ministry, and all else. One danger of this approach is that we could undermine the mystery of God's presence in worship through overanalysis. Yet, given the crisis of Christian catechesis and discipleship today, an approach that reclaims the historic significance of Christian worship is imperative.

The early Christian church, in its rites of initiation, practiced what was called an "arcane discipline." This refers to the gradual disclosure of Christian truth to converts in an extended catechetical process. The church led initiates step by step ever more deeply into knowledge of Christian teaching. Initially, inquirers to the faith were even dismissed from worship prior to the Eucharist liturgy. There remained ever deeper mysteries of the faith to learn and explore. Outsiders to the church had little awareness of or appreciation for the depths of Christian teaching. We would do well to recover a measure of arcane discipline in our own approach to worship. Contrary to the prevalent notion that the liturgy is repetitive and "boring," there are treasures buried here that the uniniti- ated cannot begin to discover. Contained in the historic order of Christian worship is an agenda for congregational ministry to last an eternity.

FOR FURTHER READING

Carroll, Jackson W. *God's Potters: Pastoral Leadership and the Shaping of Congregations*. Grand Rapids: Eerdmans, 2006.

Clapp, Rodney. *A Peculiar People: The Church as Culture in a Post-Christian Society*. Downers Grove, Ill.: InterVarsity, 1996.

Dulles, Avery. *Models of the Church*. Expanded Edition. New York: Image, 2002.

Everist, Norma Cook, and Craig L. Nessan. *Transforming Leadership: New Vision for a Church in Mission*. Minneapolis: Fortress Press, 2008.

Frambach, Nathan C. P. *Emerging Ministry: Being Church Today*. Minne- apolis: Augsburg Fortress, 2007.

Fryer, Kelly. *Recovering the "C" Word: Daring to Be Church Again*. Minne- apolis: Augsburg Fortress, 2006.

Hanover Report of the Anglican-Lutheran International Commission. *The Diaconate as Ecumenical Opportunity*. London: Anglican Commu- nion Publications, 1996.

Kiefert, Patrick R. *We Are Here Now: A New Missional Era.* Eagle, Idaho: Allelon, 2006.

Küng, Hans. *The Church.* New York: Sheed & Ward, 1967.

Mayer, David P. *Our Gifts: Identifying and Developing Leaders.* Minneapolis: Augsburg Fortress, 2002.

Rouse, Rick, and Craig Van Gelder. *A Field Guide for Missional Congregations: Embarking on a Journey of Transformation.* Minneapolis: Augsburg Fortress, 2008.

Schwarz, Hans. *The Christian Church: Biblical Origin, Historical Transformation, and Potential for the Future.* Minneapolis: Augsburg Publishing House, 1982.

Snow, Luther K. *The Power of Asset Mapping: How Your Congregation Can Act on Its Gifts.* Herndon, Va.: Alban Institute, 2004.

FOR REFLECTION AND DISCUSSION

1. What has God been doing in your congregation? Describe three areas of your congregation's life where you see God at work.

2. How does your congregation demonstrate the historic Christian practices of *kerygma*, *koinōnia*, and *diakonia*? Give specific examples.

3. Considering the nine components of a theology of the congregation (worship, prayer, education, fellowship, stewardship, evangelizing, global connections, ecumenism, and social ministry), what is working well in your congregation? How can you celebrate what is going well and build upon it?

4. Is worship mainly about what God is doing or what we are doing? When you gather for worship, how do you understand what God is doing in the worship service?

5. Why are many congregations turning to alternative and contemporary styles of worship? What is gained and what might be lost in such changes?

Chapter Two

First, Listen

If the greatest of all spiritual gifts is love, then one of the purest expressions of love is to listen. In the words of Paul Tillich, "The first duty of love is to listen." Children need it. Spouses need it. Friends need it. You need it. And the church needs it. Before one begins to lead a congregation, one should listen carefully to that congregation's story. This means listening carefully to the stories of individuals and families. But it also means listening to the story of the congregation itself. Each congregation has its own unique biography—stories of birth, growth, adolescence, maturity, and age.

Our listening to one another is grounded in God's faithful listening to us. We trust that God is always faithful to listen to our prayers, whether they come in the form of private devotions or public intercessions at worship. The Psalms, as the "prayer book of the Bible" (Bonhoeffer), instruct us that God does not discriminate among prayers according to their content. We are free to direct to God our deepest thoughts and emotions, even those of anger and vengeance. As God is patient in listening to our cries, so we as the church have the responsibility to listen to the deepest concerns shared with us by our neighbor.

In this chapter we first examine the value of listening to a congregation's story. We continue by situating the congregational story within the larger context of our culture. Finally, we locate both congregation and culture in the largest story of all, the biblical story of God's love for humanity.

Congregational Story

First impressions are not always correct. Before attempting to introduce significant change, a congregational leader honors a people by genuinely seeking to understand why things are the way they are. What has God been doing in this community? What is the extant "theology" of this congregation? How is God's activity reflected in the particular beliefs and practices of this parish? Who are the primary articulators of the congregation's theology? Are there dissenting viewpoints? What are the latent convictions and hopes awaiting future expression?

If one wants to learn the theology of a particular place and people, one must set aside plenty of time for visitation. While this visiting can take place either formally in face-to-face meetings or informally around the church, attention needs to be paid not only to the concerns of individuals but to how people express their understanding of the collective life of the congregation itself. Furthermore, people need to be invited to respond to questions about how they see God working in their church. Where has God been powerfully present for them? Where do they believe the congregation could more effectively manifest God's involvement? How do they hope God might employ this congregation in the future?

Not only is it essential to talk together about the role of a particular congregation in God's ministry, but listening also involves paying attention to "how" a congregation goes about the work of ministry. The style of worship, for example, says much about a congregation's belief in the nature and purposes of God. How a congregation conducts its meetings and makes decisions also is indicative of its operative theology. If there is a written history of the congregation, this contains invaluable information about its official self-understanding. A written history can be tested against the viewpoints of long-standing members of the congregation to test whether this is an accurate interpretation of the past. Mission statements, annual reports, and budget priorities give added insight into a congregation's theology. One can even look to the wider community to ask members and leaders of other churches about the reputation of a given church as a steward of God's grace.

Inviting others to explore together a given congregation's theology can assist members to begin asking the right questions about the congregation's identity and mission. Basic elements of a congregation's theology are reflected in how it answers basic questions about the faith:

1. What is the nature of sin? Which are the most threatening sins?
2. Which metaphors best describe Jesus?
3. What is the nature of the salvation Jesus brings?
4. What are the most important tasks of the church?
5. What is the gospel? How does one best communicate it today?
6. What importance should the sacraments have in the church?
7. What is the purpose of confirmation?
8. How involved should the church be in social issues?
9. What is the meaning of stewardship?
10. What do Christians hope for beyond death?

Implicit behind everything a congregation decides and does is a particular notion of God and God's dealings with people. There may be some significant discrepancies between what is professed and what is practiced. Congregations are no different from individual persons in this regard.

Expert resources have been written and are available to assist the inquirer in the process of discerning the character and extant theology of a particular congregation. The field of congregational studies offers tools for conducting basic ethnographic research in the congregation, investigating documents and artifacts, conducting interviews and participant observation. Learning how to examine a congregation through the lens of "local theologies" helps instruct how to listen carefully to what is being expressed not only in words but in practice. A family systems model may likewise do much to reveal the inner dynamics of a congregation's life. Preparing a congregational genotype can offer great insight.

In every case, a congregation will be enhanced by deliberate examination of its theology. By asking the right questions about where a congregation has been, is presently, and hopes to be going, the orientation shifts in the direction of mission. People are reminded that above all *God has a mission* and that Christian congregations are to place themselves in league with that mission as their very reason for existence.

Cultural Story

Congregations do not exist in a vacuum but are situated inextricably in a culture. On a continent so vast as North America, there are numerous cultural influences that impinge upon congregational life, some global, some regional, some local. In what follows, only the broadest strokes can be employed to paint a picture of "American" culture. Special reference will be made to the descriptions provided by Douglas John Hall and Tex Sample.

Douglas John Hall, in his book *Thinking the Faith*, analyzes the North American context according to seven characteristics: the end of the Constantinian era; religious pluralism; the theological impact of Auschwitz, Marxism, and the revolution of the oppressed; the nuclear crisis; the rebellion of nature; and apocalyptic consciousness with the rise of religious simplism. These categories provide a large-scale framework for commenting on the global context in which North American congregations operate.

The end of the Constantinian era for the church and the impact of religious pluralism go hand in hand. Since the fourth Christian century, the church in the West has enjoyed the luxury of having Christianity as the implicit, and often explicit, religion of the culture. In the United States, although there has been a legal separation of church and state, churches have been expected to provide religious sanction to affairs of state and have in turn received preferential status. Robert Bellah, among others, has analyzed the shape of an American civil religion that undergirds political life, which blends indistinguishably into congregational belief and practice.

The church's position in society has been further altered with the emergence of multiform religious currents. Diana Eck has described how

America has become the most religiously diverse nation on earth. Increasingly, Christianity finds itself as merely one religious option among many others. Its favored status has been challenged not only by a variety of religious competitors but also by the questionable value of religion itself in the eyes of many Americans (Charles Taylor). With much evidence, many intellectuals have heralded the dawning of a new era in the West, adorning it with the name "post-Christian."

The specter of Auschwitz continues to haunt the Christian church. The failure of the church to stand up to the moral and political challenge of Jewish genocide raises profound questions about the church's moral fiber. Christians failed not only by looking the other way but by active complicity in the arrest and execution of Jews. Is the church inherently anti-Semitic? The rise of ever new forms of anti-Jewish religion (for example, Christian Identity) in the heartland of the United States demonstrates that the church must continue to articulate its mission in a way that honors Judaism. In North America, this raises the consequent question about the church's integrity in the face of radical evil as it continues to become manifest in world affairs.

After the fall of the Berlin Wall in 1989, the fear of both Marxism and nuclear peril began to subside in American consciousness. With the rise of terrorism and the attacks of September 11, 2001, however, our endangered status has attained an acute and unprecedented level of consciousness. What abides through the decades is both the reality of the world's poor majority and the threat of violence, even the use of nuclear weapons, by those gripped by a fervent ideology. As the root cause of the world's instability are the millions of people who do not have enough to eat or the material sufficiency to survive. Those who turn to violence often do so with a sense of righteous indignation at the injustice of it all. Such causes become perilous in an age of nuclear weapons.

Concern for the natural environment grows in the awareness of many Americans. Not only the importance of recycling but the dilemmas of resource depletion and waste disposal, which are unprecedented in previous generations, deserve priority on the church's agenda. Human beings are increasingly challenged to see themselves not above but within the complex web of life which we call the ecosystem. Human flourishing can no longer take place at the expense of the natural world, but rather human beings must understand themselves as part of the natural world, indeed that part exclusively responsible for the present disequilibrium.

Finally, there is the strong temptation in an immensely complex world to reduce issues to simple formulas. Religious people are often tempted to take refuge in an apocalyptic outlook that sees the only possible resolution to contemporary crises in the dramatic intervention of God in human history to punish the guilty and reward the faithful. Security is sought in the certainty of authority, whether from Scripture or charismatic leaders, who are believed to shelter the faithful from the corruption of the decaying order. The consequences of such retreats from engagement are twofold: defense of the status quo (lest any further erosion take place) and passivity in addressing the imperatives of the future.

If Hall provides helpful contours for situating North America in the global context, Tex Sample, in his book *U.S. Lifestyles and Mainline Churches*, provides a guide for understanding some of the more subtle dynamics of American culture. Sample's analysis of American society is helpful in that he distinguishes between a "cultural left," "cultural right," and "cultural middle." Each of these groupings are further subdivided and characterized.

The cultural left is notable for the self-directedness of its ambitions, its relative affluence, and the value it places on personal choice and tolerance. Rejecting the perceived conformism of previous generations, the cultural left establishes its own priorities and agendas with wariness toward external authority. Benefiting from the affluence of the previous generation, however, the cultural left has acquired formidable educational credentials, which secure its own economic status. Extraordinarily high value is placed upon freedom of choice in all matters of lifestyle, including religious preference. The only trait not tolerated is intolerance itself.

The cultural left can itself be divided into three subgroups: the "I-am-mes," the "Experientials," and the "Societally Conscious." The "I-am-mes" operate with a decided preference for novelty in their self-expression and tend to be the cultural left's youngest members. The "Experientials" focus on their own participation in unique life-experience, whether it be of the natural world, chemically-induced, or mystical. The "Societally Conscious" are at the forefront of movements for social and political change. Environmental activism, social justice advocacy, and world peace are major concerns. Within the purview of the cultural left falls also the New Age movement, with its interest in a holistic approach to self, others, society, nature, and the divine.

The cultural right, by contrast, is characterized by concern for providing life's basic necessities and by rootedness in a specific locale. Due to their imperiled economic status, members of the cultural right devote the major portion of their lives to securing food, shelter, and whatever niceties can be afforded. The most cherished value is what contributes to the well-being of the family. An ethos of the local community and neighborhood prevails, providing the parameters for this worldview.

The cultural right can also be subdivided into three categories: the "Respectables," the "Hard Living," and the "Desperate Poor." The "Respectables" constitutes the largest portion of the cultural right. While occupational, and thus economic, advancement is limited by education and training, this group places great emphasis on leading a decent and respectable life within the given parameters. Of all the subdivisions of American culture, this one is the largest and the most threatened during times of economic recession. This group is likely the backbone of many Christian congregations.

The "Hard Living" consists of those hardy individuals whose lifestyles entail heavy labor and often heavy drinking. This group tends to live for today without concern for tomorrow. There prevails an overriding sense of powerlessness, which translates all too often into marital strife and domestic violence. The "Desperate Poor" includes both those locked in vicious cycles of intergenerational poverty and those who through age or misfortune cannot provide sufficiently for themselves.

The cultural right adheres to popular forms of religion and conventional morality. God's providence shapes the course of daily events. There is tremendous respect and authority lent to mediators of religious truth, both clergy and Scripture. Churches offer a strong sense of community that reinforces the prevailing values of the local setting. Personal devotion, expressed through confidence in the power of prayer to solve problems and the comfort of religious objects, is common. Going to church and loving one's country are integral to a respectable life.

The cultural middle places career at the center of existence. Successful members of this group have completed higher education and find themselves situated in jobs that offer a high level of satisfaction. In order to maximize their achievements in career, this group is typically mobile and places relatively little value on place or community. They are of necessity individualists who are frequently willing to postpone gratification to a later time in order to excel in their work. Spouses and families, while providing a base of support, must also be willing to make sacrifices for the sake of career advancement.

Again, the cultural middle can be divided into three subcategories: the "Successful," the "Strivers," and the "Conflicted." The "Successful" are those who are living out the American dream. Happy in their work, well-compensated, and able to afford the good things money can buy, this subgroup consists of business executives, lawyers, physicians, politicians, and others who set the standards for "the good life." The "Strivers" aspire to the lifestyle of the "Successful" but, lacking either the opportunity or the skills, never quite make the grade. This subgroup, often leveling out in midmanagement positions, nevertheless attempts to keep up with the upper echelon and often falls into serious debt in the process.

The third subcategory consists of the "Conflicted," those caught between aspirations of career and commitment to their families. These do not fully share the willingness to sacrifice family stability for the sake of career achievement. At the same time, they are not ready to settle down in a lifestyle of respectability without affluence. However, their career paths make it likely they will never ascend toward a higher standard of living. They are indeed caught in an irreconcilable conflict of values, leading to much frustration.

The religious leanings of the cultural middle are toward beliefs and practices that reinforce and provide legitimation for their position in society. Faith finds its proper orbit circling the personal needs of the individual. Success in career tends to be interpreted as a sign of God's blessing. Insofar as the corporate dimension is important, the church serves to support the individual's immediate family and provides an interesting array of enrichment opportunities. The cultural middle places strong reservations on the role of the church in initiating social change. Ministering to the needs of the destitute is appropriate but not by advocating structural change. Members of the cultural middle are likely to hold positions of leadership in the church where their management and organization skills can be put to good use.

Sample's breakdown of American culture into a left, right, and middle provides a helpful lens for considering the theology of a particular congregation. Each congregation consists of its own peculiar mix of cultural styles. Depending on the particular constituency, the theological perspective will vary. This means that leadership in a particular parish will need to take seriously both the proclivities and weaknesses of the cultural persuasions of its members as it builds its theological vision. To fail to reckon with prevailing attitudes means working at a disadvantage, if not dooming one to unproductive conflict. While this book proposes a particular model for imagining a theology of the congregation, the particular ideas will always require adaptation to meet local circumstances.

Neither Hall nor Sample touches on every aspect of American culture. For example, the ubiquity of media in shaping popular opinion has hardly been mentioned. Consumerism remains a major competitor with religion for ultimate allegiance. Likewise, the changes in the American economy toward jobs primarily in the service sector and the problems of under- and unemployment have only been indirectly addressed. The reader is invited to bring to this discussion his or her own cultural critique as it contributes to a fuller understanding of the context in which the local congregation does ministry.

Biblical Story

The story of a congregation does not begin with its local history nor end with its location in a particular culture. Instead, the story of every Christian congregation begins with God's first Word spoken at creation and ends with the consummation of all things in God's eternity. It is vital that a congregation see itself in the perspective of God's own story, lest it stray from its God-given identity and mission.

This story begins with the wisdom of the God who freely decided to create a universe, including creatures to whom God entrusted a mind of their own. These creatures, humankind, although made for a unique relationship with God as those made in God's very own image, are responsible for profound and wanton rebellion against their maker. In choosing to follow after other gods, they lose not only the source of their very life but their own peace of mind. As a consequence, their relationships with others become severely troubled, even to the point of violence and war.

God, being compassionate and merciful, did not abandon humanity to its own self-destruction. Instead, God sends messenger after messenger with warning of ruin should they continue on their current path, and with promise of grace, even when they fail to heed the warning. Abraham and Sarah, Moses and Miriam, Deborah and Isaiah, Ezra and Esther, each have left testimony to God's faithfulness. The people of Israel are God's chosen ones for bringing God's teachings and God's mercy to the entire world.

The Jews had long anticipated a Messiah who would usher in God's perfect kingdom of justice and peace. In the fullness of time, God sent a son into the world, born of Mary, to incarnate divine truth. Jesus preached and taught God's kingdom. God is not distant but near. God is not severe but merciful. By the telling of provocative and captivating stories, Jesus revealed the nature of God's presence in the world. The sick were healed by his touch. Disciples were called into community. Sinners, forgiven, were welcomed home. The distinction between righteous and unrighteous, clean and unclean, insider and outsider, Jew and Gentile, was erased in table fellowship with Jesus. The love he demonstrated broke all rules of propriety and threatened to disrupt the social order. Jesus died on the cross and was raised to new life on Easter. Doubting disciples heard, saw, and believed. God chose the foolishness of Jesus' death on the cross to inaugurate an age in which all people would hear the gospel, receive forgiveness of sins, and hope for the promise of resurrection life after death. All these gifts are ours for Jesus' sake.

God gave the Holy Spirit to the church that it might follow the way of Jesus and proclaim the gospel of forgiveness and love to all. For two thousand years the church has struggled to remain faithful to this calling. At times the church has been willing to sacrifice much, even life itself, for the cause of Jesus. At other times the church has virtually forgotten its identity and mission. The history of the church—the age of the martyrs, the triumph of Christendom, the witness of reformers, and the challenges of the contemporary world—provides much seed for its thought and practice as the church continues to search for orientation today.

The Christian congregation, whose building is located on a particular street corner or highway and whose members are influenced by the rapidly changing currents of American culture, must see itself in the larger perspective of God's dealings with humanity through Israel, Jesus, and the history of the church. The mission entrusted to the people of God in ages past belongs now to the church today and thereby to every congregation.

We are to be the people who name ourselves with the name of Jesus. Our *identity* is of those for whom Jesus died. We are to gather together to worship and learn and befriend one another for the purpose of remembering Jesus. We employ the gifts God has given us in thankful service. For Jesus' sake we are forgiven and have the hope of eternal life.

In the same way, we are people with a purpose. Our *mission* is to share the good news by which we ourselves are identified. By word of mouth we tell others about the treasure that is ours in Christ and invite them to come into our midst in the Christian congregation. We seek to build ecumenical bridges with other Christian people from whom we are estranged. We seek to link our lives ever more intentionally with Christian people across the globe. We explore what it means to be generous in a world of need and peacemakers in a world of violence. All of this we do in order that the gospel of Christ might be believed and the kingdom Jesus proclaimed might be present. Wherever governments, corporations, or other powers contradict the rule of Christ, there the church summons its wisdom and courage to respond faithfully.

While as leaders in the church we begin by listening to the theology of the local congregation and pay attention to the strictures of the culture in which the church finds itself, we must also remain steadfast to God's own story as it has unfolded over the ages. We must claim this story ever anew as our own heritage. If we fail to claim our true identity and respond to our God-given mission, the cause is lost.

FOR FURTHER READING

Ammerman, Nancy Tatom, Jackson W. Carroll, Carl S. Dudley, and William McKinney, eds. *Studying Congregations: A New Handbook.* Nashville: Abingdon, 1998.

Bellah, Robert N., Richard Madsen, William M. Sullivan, and Ann Swidler. *Habits of the Heart: Individualism and Commitment in American Life.* Third Edition. Berkeley: University of California Press, 2007.

Bevans, Stephen B. *Models of Contextual Theology.* Revised and Expanded Edition. Maryknoll, N.Y.: Orbis, 2002.

Daubert, Dave. *Living Lutheran: Renewing Your Congregation.* Minneapolis: Augsburg Fortress, 2007.

Eck, Diana L. *A New Religious America: How a "Christian Country" Has Become the World's Most Religiously Diverse Nation.* New York: HarperCollins, 2002.

Hall, Douglas John. *The Cross in Our Context: Jesus and the Suffering of the World.* Minneapolis: Augsburg Fortress, 2003.

Hopewell, James F. *Congregation: Stories and Structures.* Philadelphia: Fortress Press, 1987.

Nieman, James R. *Knowing the Context: Frames, Tools, and Signs for Preaching.* Minneapolis: Fortress Press, 2008.

Sample, Tex. *U.S. Lifestyles and Mainline Churches.* Louisville: Westminster John Knox, 1990.

Schreiter, Robert. *Constructing Local Theologies.* Maryknoll, N.Y.: Orbis, 1985.

Steinke, Peter L. *How Your Church Family Works: Understanding Congregations as Emotional Systems.* Herndon, Va.: Alban Institute, 2006.

Taylor, Charles. *A Secular Age.* Cambridge, Mass.: Belknap, 2007.

Wuthnow, Robert. *America and the Challenges of Religious Diversity.* Princeton: Princeton University Press, 2005.

FOR REFLECTION AND DISCUSSION

1. What helps you to be a good listener to others?
2. What are the most important insights you have gained from observing and listening to the story of your congregation?
3. What methods might your congregation employ to deepen its wisdom about its identity and mission?
4. What are the chief characteristics of American and global culture that are affecting your congregation in the present?
5. When you reflect on the span of God's story in the Bible and church history, what connections do you see with the life of your congregation in the present time?

Chapter Three

Trinitarian Mission: The Sending of the Son in the Power of the Spirit

The mission of the Holy Trinity undergirds this theology of the congregation. First, we pay attention to the God whose rule Jesus proclaimed at the heart of his message. We seek to reinvigorate congregational self-understanding with reference to the language of Jesus and the metaphor of the kingdom of God. One of the most exciting trends in New Testament study is the rediscovery of what Jesus meant by the *kingdom*. The language Jesus used to describe God and God's activity, especially in his parables, informs our understanding of God's continuing involvement in the world today. Jesus' understanding of the kingdom reminds us that God is near and God is merciful. The wisdom of this God is a subversive wisdom.

Second, with reference to Christology, we draw upon Luther's insistence upon the *real presence* of Christ in Word and Sacrament. It is the crucified and risen Jesus Christ who is still alive to meet us when we gather together in worship for the sake of the gospel. Only as we trust that Christ is as alive among us as he was in earlier generations do we recognize the vital importance of what we do as Christian congregations.

Third, with regard to the Holy Spirit, we refer to the inexorable movement, demonstrated especially clearly in the letters of Paul, from proclamation of the gospel to *paraenesis*, that is, a life lived in conformity to the way of Jesus Christ. While our justification is solely by grace through faith in Christ, the Holy Spirit continues to enliven the church with gifts freshly incarnated in the lives of believers. Together the members of a congregation are the body of Christ in a certain time and place. The gospel sets us free for a life lived "in Christ."

After developing this trinitarian foundation, we continue in the next chapter with the theme of worship in constructing a theology that serves both the identity and the mission of the congregation. Jesus Christ remains the cornerstone for the entire structure.

Jesus and the Kingdom of God

Jesus spoke of God's interaction with humankind in terms of "the kingdom." Both his aphorisms and his parables testify to a profound faith in the nearness and mercy of God given characteristic expression by this symbol.

Today there are those who hesitate to employ the term *kingdom* because of its patriarchal connotations or out of fear that it is inseparable from an antiquated and oppressive social system. Those so inclined may take comfort in alternative translations of basileía toû theoû: rule of God, commonwealth of God, fellowship of God, or even friendship of God. In recent years I have experimented also with other new metaphors, speaking of the kingdom as the "dream of God" or the "culture of God." Each of these translations adds new insight into what Jesus meant by the kingdom. However, I will primarily employ the more literal translation, kingdom of God, precisely because what Jesus means by kingdom inverts the standards of success and power commonly regnant in human affairs. This translation also preserves the political weight of what Jesus was talking about.

Kingdom does not refer to a locale in time or space but to a particular mode of God's activity. While the full arrival of God's kingdom awaits future consummation, what is daring about Jesus' teachings is the claim that the kingdom already impinges upon the present, indeed *the kingdom is the single most important reality determining human life.* The kingdom is present as Jesus casts out demons (Luke 11:20). The arrival of the kingdom is not measured by calculating signs but is already "in the midst of you" (Luke 17:20-21). The kingdom suffers violence at the hands of those who would seize it by force (Matt 11:12).

The teachings of Jesus, particularly his parables, demonstrate that where God rules, there is a dramatic reversal of expectations and values. Like the one discovering buried treasure in a field, the one who discovers the kingdom acquires immeasurable joy (Matt 13:44). The kingdom lacks all sense of measure in apportioning forgiveness (Luke 15:11-32, Prodigal Son). There is urgency about the affairs of the kingdom that requires leaving other matters behind (Matt 22:1-14, the Great Supper). Fairness yields to mercy in the kingdom (Matt 20:1-16, Laborers in the Vineyard). Mercy draws near from an unimaginable source (Luke 10:29-37, Good Samaritan). God is the origin of mercy that surpasses every human example (Luke 18:1-8, the Unjust Judge). The increase of the kingdom, though mysterious, is guaranteed through the power of God (Mark 4:3-9, the Sower).

Though these sketches of the parables are far too brief, they serve to underscore the nature of the kingdom that Jesus announced. Furthermore, *the life of Jesus* depicts actions fully consistent with the view of the kingdom articulated in the parables. In the kingdom, all are welcome: children, women, unclean lepers, the demon-possessed, Gentiles, tax collectors, and public sinners. In the kingdom, the hungry are fed. Nowhere were the values of the kingdom more evident than in the table fellowship of Jesus. Disciple and opponent alike looked askance at the company Jesus kept and at the scandalous people he invited to dinner. It is fitting that it was at such table fellowship the night before his death that Jesus instituted a meal for his remembrance. Even from the cross, Jesus testified to the mercy of the kingdom, inviting into paradise a penitent thief and praying for forgiveness for those who executed him.

The kingdom of God that Jesus both taught and embodied revolves around two central convictions: *God is near* and *God is merciful.* God is not distant and detached from human affairs but near, involved, connected. The reality of the kingdom is "in, with, and under" the reality of the everyday, for those with the eyes to perceive. Jesus' life of prayer and his peculiar address for God as Abba—"Daddy," "Papa"—demonstrate a vivid sense of God's nearness and presence. At the same time this familial term for God communicates Jesus' assurance that God is merciful. God is not severe and condemning, but invites and welcomes the sinner home. Jesus imparted this awareness of God's proximity and loving-kindness to his disciples as he taught them to pray and to live the Lord's Prayer: "Our Father . . . your kingdom come . . . forgive us our sins . . . as we forgive."

Marcus Borg, in his book *Jesus: A New Vision: Spirit, Culture, and the Life of Discipleship*, presents the case that the kingdom of God as proclaimed by Jesus runs counter to the precepts of conventional wisdom, now as well as then. Conventional wisdom operates with well-defined notions of family, wealth, honor, and religion. Family lines are carefully delineated; obligations of blood kinship have primacy; family structure is patriarchal. Wealth is a sign of God's favor, poverty a sign of divine absence or punishment. Honor comes to those with status and power over others; they command preferential treatment, especially when in the public eye. Religion is a matter of maintaining purity, that is, living a good life according to the prevailing mores.

The kingdom envisioned by Jesus contradicts each of these maxims of conventional wisdom. Regarding family, all are brothers and sisters under the parenthood of God in the kingdom. The community of Jesus is scandalously egalitarian. In the kingdom, true wealth consists of trust in God, not mammon. The least of the brothers and the sisters are the honored ones in the kingdom. The greatest must be the servants of all. Religion requires neither purity nor performance but faith in the nearness and compassion of the living God in the kingdom. The wisdom of Jesus is subversive of conventional standards on all decisive points. *Is it any wonder that this man's life ended in crucifixion?!*

The kingdom which Jesus proclaimed and embodied was called into radical question by his death. The disciples scattered in fear. Jesus' enemies triumphed. He had been eliminated. Conventional wisdom prevailed, then as now. The rich get richer; the poor get poorer. The rest pay taxes to Caesar. All is right with the conventional world. Until Easter, that is.

The resurrection of Jesus, however, means nothing is as it appears. The power of guilt to cripple is overcome by the forgiveness of sins granted by the superior power of the cross. The grip of evil—of Satan—is broken by the stronger grip of God's love. Even that which seems most certain of all, the reality of death, loses its control as God raised Jesus from the dead. With Jesus' resurrection, this promise is extended: all those who trust in Jesus, and thereby in the kingdom for which he stands, will share in his victory over sin, Satan, and death itself. Life in the kingdom, eternal life, is what lasts forever.

This construal of the life, teachings, death, and resurrection of Jesus, revolving around his vision of God's imminent and gracious kingdom, provides a first and essential point of reference for the theology of the congregation to follow. Keep in mind the kingdom!

Living Word of Gospel

Luther and the Reformers in the sixteenth century sought to recover a vivid awareness of the involvement of God in human life, the very incarnation of God in the human flesh of Jesus. In or outside of the church building, God's involvement means grace. In particular, the strictures of conventional religious wisdom, given expression at that time through a host of pious customs (not least the sale of certificates of pardon called indulgences), were forced to yield to Scripture's central message of God's unconditional love and pure grace revealed in the person of Jesus.

For Luther as for Paul, the nature of God's love was nowhere more profoundly (although paradoxically) revealed than in the wisdom of the cross. Luther clung to a *theology of the cross* over against all the theologies of glory that vie for human allegiance. God does not abandon us in time of trial, loss, and grief. Rather, because of the cross, we dare to believe that God is mysteriously present with us at exactly those times it would be easiest to despair. It is not by our own merit or works, our own performance, that we attain God's favor. Solely for the sake of the sufferings of Jesus and by the grace of his resurrection we dare to hope for eternal life. All this is ours "by faith in the Son of God who loved me and gave himself for me" (Luther's Small Catechism).

The central theological concern of the Reformation demonstrates *striking congruity with Jesus' message of the kingdom*. While focus definitely shifts from a Galilean's trusting response to the teaching of Jesus, to a German's faith in the person and works of Jesus, the content remains remarkably consistent. That content is summarized in a single word: *gospel*! The good news preached by Jesus: the kingdom of God is at hand, nearby and gracious! The gospel according to the Reformers: sins are forgiven and eternal life won by the death and resurrection of Christ! Both messages resound joyously in the ears and hearts of those estranged from God by virtue of their own guilt and fear. Both draw the believer near again to God, working reconciliation. Both liberate the captive, setting one free to love the neighbor.

The power of the gospel is derived from *the living presence of the crucified and risen Christ who comes to us in Word and Sacrament*. Luther's theology differed from late medieval piety in its shift away from fearful observance of religious rituals and the magical practice of religious customs. Instead, Luther insisted upon an actual encounter with a gracious God in Jesus Christ. "Word" for Luther consisted not only of the reading of holy Scripture at worship but especially of preaching, which becomes God's living Word for us today, convicting us of our sin and recreating us by the power of Christ.

Regarding the sacraments, Luther was unshakable in his conviction that *Christ is really present in the acts of Baptism and Holy Communion*. God employs the most common elements of the earth in service of the gospel—water, bread, wine—and attaches to them a living word of promise. Just as God became incarnate in the flesh and blood of Jesus, so now Christ is actually present in the sacraments. Particularly in his dispute with Zwingli over the nature of Christ's presence in the bread and wine, Luther demonstrated a deep commitment to sacramental realism. Christ says the bread and wine are his body and blood, and so they are. The nature of Christ's presence, moreover, does not mean condemnation but forgiveness, grace, and new life, wrought by Christ himself.

This theology is wonderfully summarized in the seventh article of the Augsburg Confession concerning the church: "This is the assembly of all believers among whom the Gospel is preached in its purity and the holy sacraments are administered according to the Gospel." To risk a rough paraphrase, the church is where believers "have it done to them" by the gospel in preaching and sacraments. This means that *God is the most important actor in what takes place at worship.* It is this confessional conviction that is greatly at risk when we spurn a sacramental understanding of worship in favor of what is most appealing to us as consumers.

Permeating Luther's view of worship, preaching, and the sacraments is a vivid theology of the Holy Spirit. The Holy Spirit operates in fulfillment of God's promises as the Word of God is proclaimed and the sacraments are celebrated. By the power of the Holy Spirit, Christ is made present in the sacramental event. One can depend on Christ's presence because a special promise has been attached by God to these means of grace. Regin Prenter has described Luther's view as one of "dynamic realism." Christ is "really present" to accomplish God's work of redemption. This presence is "dynamic" insofar as Christ actually does something in the encounter. Sins are forgiven. Lives are changed. Eternal life is received.

All of the revisions in worship that Luther advocated in the sixteenth century were in service of an enhanced appreciation for the living presence of Christ. Worship in the vernacular made it possible for worshipers to meet Christ in their own language. When the Word was preached, it was God who did the speaking, through the preacher. Congregational singing is an expression of gratitude not only for what God has done but for what God is continuing to accomplish among those assembled. The people participate in Holy Communion, themselves receiving the sacrament in both kinds. Only so do they meet the living Christ, who bears gifts of salvation and whom they receive in faith.

Jesus' embodiment of the kingdom and Luther's defense of Christ's real and living presence in Word and Sacrament, taken together, provide the theological basis for rejuvenating the worship life of every Christian congregation. Yet, a third theological footing must be set. We turn next to a consideration of the movement from proclamation to *paraenesis* in the letters of Paul.

From Proclamation to *Paraenesis*

Luther and the Reformers rightly insisted that justification is the central Christian doctrine by which the church stands or falls. Those who remain confused about the central truth that we are made right with God by grace alone through faith alone have consciences that are burdened and lives that are driven by compulsions of various sorts. Luther grounded this brilliant theological insight on his reading of Paul's letter to the Romans. All have sinned and fall short of the glory of God. We are justified by Christ's death on the cross and receive God's declaration of forgiveness solely by faith. Baptism marks the death of the sinner and the raising up of the baptized as a child of God. All of life is lived henceforth under the influence of Christ, that is, "in Christ."

Wherever one begins in reading Paul—with his letter to the Romans, the theology of the cross in 1 Corinthians, or with another text—the direction of the Pauline epistles always moves inexorably toward instruction in the Christian life. Major portions of Paul's letters are devoted to a discussion of practices that raise challenges for Christian existence in the world. The exhortation and instruction for the Christian life found in the New Testament is sometimes called *paraenesis*. While major attention has usually focused on the doctrinal elements in Paul's writings, the inexorable drive toward *paraenesis* receives relatively scant comment. The paraenetic element, however, provides crucial direction for a theology of the congregation.

One must keep in mind that the communities that Paul instructed in his letters all gathered together regularly for worship. Within their own cultures, these Christian churches were suspected of scandal; they were followers of an odd and sectarian deity. As with the situation of minority people today, every aspect of life was subject to public scrutiny. This meant that Christian testimony consisted not only of a message spoken aloud to others about Jesus Christ ("talking the talk") but also was measured by the quality of the life led by those known to be followers of Jesus ("walking the walk").

For Paul, the sphere of Christ's influence extended over the entirety of life. In effect, either one is under the sway of Christ or one is not. "The way of the flesh" (*katà sárka*) is Paul's characteristic designation for a life lived in opposition to Christ. "The way of the Spirit" (*katà pneuma*), by contrast, describes a life consistent with the gospel. The tension between these two ways remains an ongoing challenge, even for Christians. The power of sin continues to afflict those who belong to Christ. Yet the Spirit of God is ever present to re-create and direct the lives of the baptized.

The letter to the Romans provides a sterling example of how Paul's theology leads to a transformed lifestyle. Chapters 1–3 argue for the universality of sin; Jew and Gentile alike are condemned. Justification takes place by faith alone by the power of Christ's death on the cross (Rom 4–5). In baptism, we are incorporated into Christ's death and resurrection, which become for us the source of new life (Rom 6). This does not mean we ever become free of sin (Rom 7), but by the power of God's Spirit at work in us, we are in the process of being transformed (Rom 8).

After an exploration of the problem of Israel's provisional disbelief in Christ (Rom 9–11), Paul concludes the letter with extensive instructions for the Christian life (Rom 12–16). Similar concerns are discussed at length in virtually every one of his epistles. Chapter 12 begins: "I appeal to you therefore, brothers and sisters, by the mercies of God, to present your bodies as a living sacrifice, holy and acceptable to God, which is your spiritual worship. Do not be conformed to this world, but be transformed by the renewing of your minds, so that you may discern what is the will of God—what is good and acceptable and perfect." The remainder of the letter deals with matters of the Christian lifestyle.

Paul elaborated in both general and specific terms to address the requisites of a life lived in Christ. Consistently, Paul dealt with issues of reconciliation within the community, response to civil authority, the appropriate response to pagan religious practices, sexual ethics, and the law of love for one's neighbor. Though our context is separated significantly in time and space, the dilemmas we face are strikingly analogous as we seek to follow the way of Christ in our lives today. Paul exhorted the recipients of his letters to conform their lives to the image of Christ. Sometimes he gave very specific details about what this should mean in a particular situation. More frequently, however, Paul pointed out a direction to be followed in the spirit of Christ.

While the exact dilemmas facing those early Christians are not our
own, nevertheless, we are summoned to examine our own lives and measure them according to the way of Jesus Christ. Without becoming bound
up by legalism, we too are summoned to let the spirit of Christ rule in
our hearts. The "epistle of our lives" continues to witness to others about
what we say we believe. Love for the neighbor remains the standard Christ
left us by which to measure our lives. In our own individual piety, in the
Christian *koinōnia*, and in the public square, we are made free by the
gospel of justification by grace to live out our faith in the way of Christ.
When we set out in false directions, the opinion of the whole counsel of
God and the wisdom of the Christian community provide checks on our
behavior.

Beginning with worship centered on Word and Sacrament, the Christian community moves into the world in mission. Evangelism, global
connections, ecumenism, and social ministry each derive from the same
impulse that moved Paul to *parenaesis*. The Holy Spirit of God wills not
only transformed individual lives but a transformed world.

FOR FURTHER READING

Aageson, James W. *Paul, the Pastoral Epistles, and the Early Church.* Pea-
    body, Mass.: Hendrickson, 2008.
Boff, Leonardo. *Trinity and Society.* Translated by Paul Burns. Eugene,
    Ore.: Wipf & Stock, 2005.
Borg, Marcus J. *Jesus: A New Vision: Spirit, Culture, and the Life of Disciple-
    ship.* San Francisco: HarperSanFrancisco, 1991.
Brueggemann, Walter. *The Prophetic Imagination.* Second Edition. Min-
    neapolis: Fortress Press, 2001.
Horsley, Richard A. *Jesus and Empire: The Kingdom of God and the New
    World Disorder.* Minneapolis: Fortress Press, 2002.
LaCugna, Catherine M. *God for Us: The Trinity and the Christian Life.* San
    Francisco: HarperSanFrancisco, 1993.
Madsen, Anna. *The Theology of the Cross in Historical Perspective.* Eugene,
    Ore.: Pickwick, 2007.
Meuser, Fred W. *Luther the Preacher.* Minneapolis: Augsburg, 1983.

Perrin, Norman. *Jesus and the Language of the Kingdom: Symbol and Metaphor in New Testament Interpretation*. Philadelphia: Fortress Press, 1980.

Prenter, Regin. *Spiritus Creator: Luther's Concept of the Holy Spirit*. Eugene, Ore.: Wipf & Stock, 2001.

Silberman, Neil Asher, and Richard A. Horsley. *The Message and the Kingdom: How Jesus and Paul Ignited a Revolution and Transformed the Ancient World*. Minneapolis: Fortress Press, 2002.

Vajta, Vilmos. *Luther on Worship: An Interpretation*. Eugene, Ore.: Wipf & Stock, 2004.

FOR REFLECTION AND DISCUSSION

1. Put in your own words what Jesus meant by the kingdom of God. Where in the life of the world do you see signs of God's kingdom at work today?

2. If the kingdom of God means a reversal of conventional values, where do you and your congregation experience the most tension with the unconventional values about family, wealth, honor, and religion as taught by Jesus?

3. How do you understand what Luther meant by the theology of the cross? What difference might this teaching have for the ministry and mission of your congregation?

4. How does the life of your congregation reflect the conviction that Jesus Christ is really present, as alive today as ever before in the history of the church?

5. What is the relationship between the free grace of God in Jesus Christ as the basis of our faith and how we live our lives? Where does the Holy Spirit fit into your understanding of the activity of the triune God?

Chapter Four

Worship: Imagining the Kingdom

For some it happens when playing basketball. For others it occurs contemplating great works of art, painting, or music. Among children it happens all the time. When one pretends, the boundaries between the ordinary world and the world of imagination dissolve. In fact, the world of the imagination can become so compelling that one totally forgets that any other world even exists. Try calling a child who is playing video games to come to dinner, and you may not easily connect. The reality of the cyber world may be far more compelling than anything you have to offer. Or observe with what fanaticism supposedly mature people can play a game of cards. For a person with schizophrenia, the fantasy world may not even allow a return to "reality."

These examples are offered to prepare the reader for the interpretation of worship that follows. To imagine is not to do something trivial. To imagine, in the sense here described, is to enter into *an alternative world* that can profoundly shape and alter the ordinary world. Albert Einstein has been frequently quoted as saying: "Imagination is more important than knowledge." What he meant is that the imagination has the power to so grip our awareness that our lives become forever changed.

While it is possible and important to know many things, knowledge is not what changes us. Instead, what changes us are the dreams that grip us, the idea that things do not have to be like they always have been, the power to imagine another course. Rarely have I ever changed my life based solely on facts. Rather, I am moved to change when I can imagine my life otherwise.

When theologians describe the nature of faith, usually they talk primarily about two elements: trust and belief. Faith as "trust" means that we rely upon God as the source of all goodness and life itself. Luther did much to reclaim the meaning of faith as trust, trusting in God above all things. Faith as "belief" refers to the content of what one believes. We believe in the articles of faith named in the creed, for example, God as the Creator of heaven and earth. However, there is a third dimension of faith that we neglect at our peril, that is, faith as imagination. What Jesus did in his ministry was to tell stories that invited people to imagine what it meant to have a living God who made a real difference in the way things are and the way things turn out. Jesus appealed to the human imagination to envision an alternative world, a world where God makes all things new. Imagination is the lost dimension of faith itself.

When we worship, we enter into just such an alternative world. Perhaps we take Sunday mornings so much for granted that we no longer realize what is going on. This pivotal chapter seeks to reawaken our wonder for the mystery of *what God is doing to us* as we worship. While we ourselves engage in "imagining" the kingdom of God, God is in the very act of enacting that kingdom in our midst!

In the Name of . . .

Worship commences in the name of the Father, Son, and Holy Spirit. The invocation of the divine name signals our entry into another time and space, what anthropologists call ritual time and ritual space. Of the many qualities that make for excellence in worship, none is needed more urgently than a profound sense of imagination. As one gathers for worship, one must be willing to let down one's defenses, suspend preoccupation with the "real" world and, like a child, imagine. What we imagine at worship is nothing other than the kingdom of God, the same kingdom Jesus proclaimed and lived in his earthly ministry. At the very same time that we engage in imagining the kingdom, however, our God is at work by the power of the Spirit to create that very kingdom in our lives and relationships.

Life is punctuated by rituals of many sorts, some so familiar we fail to recognize them as such. Families develop rituals of table blessing and bedtime prayers that interrupt business as usual. Our culture observes rituals rich in symbolism: Valentine's Day with its focus on love, or Halloween with its invocation of supernatural powers that haunt. The nation celebrates its mythology through the rituals of Independence Day and Thanksgiving. What each of these ritual occasions provides is the opportunity to give expression to our deepest convictions, to articulate and rehearse what we ordinarily take for granted. When we participate in ritual, the beliefs that normally remain implicit are made explicit. And the course of our lives is altered by the recognition that occurs.

Imagination rests at the heart of ritual. Those who are exceedingly self-conscious have a difficult time letting go of control and letting ritual take over. Especially in a culture where self-control is so highly valued, some may feel threatened by ritual performance. Yet in other arenas of life, there are analogies that parallel what takes place in worship. Great works of art invite us to enter into an alternative way of viewing the world, which forever alters how we ourselves see things. Games, in which we participate either as players or even as spectators, can become so gripping that we forget who and where we are apart from the playing. Drama, movies, or television programs can lead us to suspend our ordinary worries and so identify with the characters that we laugh and cry as though we are one of them.

By the power of the imagination, one is able to vivify things and people that are absent, separated by time or space. Thereby, one can become transported out of ordinary circumstances into another realm. People in our culture are hungry to imagine an alternative to this world. Evidence of this deep and desperate hunger abounds. Movies, television programs, spectator sports, virtual reality, and various New Age religious practices each offer the starving imagination nourishment. Through these and other media, the participant exits the realm of the ordinary and enters an alternative world. While dwelling in alternative time and space, the individual experiences life through the eyes of another. There is release from the tensions of the everyday. One's own life and problem become relativized. One begins to view one's own predicament in a new light. New possibilities for thought and action are afforded.

Victor Turner, in his fascinating book *The Ritual Process*, demonstrates cross-culturally the indispensable importance of ritual for life. Day by day we live in firmly established orders that provide what Turner calls "structure." Within the structure of life, however, there are hierarchies of power leading to inequity and oppression. Through ritual the ordinary world is, at least temporarily, undone. Rituals offer what Turner calls *communitas*, that is, entry into an alternative world, where the structure of ordinary life undergoes reversal. In ritual time and space, the powerful become subject to the weak, one imagines a peaceable and egalitarian alternative, vexing problems find improbable solutions, and individuals transfer through rites of passage from one life stage into another.

Turner argues that the "liminality" of ritual is a necessary corollary to the structure of ordinary life. The power relations of ordinary life exist in dialectical tension with the alternative world of ritual. In the ritual process, the power structure ruling the everyday becomes relativized. Although at the conclusion of a ritual, nothing about the ordinary structure may appear to have been altered; in fact everything is differently arranged. Insight is gained into the way things could and ought to be. The weak are lent hope, and the powerful are humbled. Problems are solved. Illnesses are healed. Passage from one status in life to another is attained.

Although people in contemporary culture demonstrate an immense hunger for ritual time and space, the church too often fails to value the gift it has to offer in feeding the human imagination. The church through its ritual resources—the church year and the historic liturgy—has nourishment that can truly satisfy the hungry heart. The church has something genuinely worthy of the human imagination—the very kingdom of God. However, instead of creatively embracing its ritual heritage, it often succumbs to the temptation of overly rationalizing the worship service or takes refuge in contemporary services far less ritually satisfying.

What we ritualize by means of the historic Christian liturgy is nothing other than the very kingdom of God proclaimed by and embodied in the person of Jesus. As we gather on Sunday morning in the name of the triune God, we enter into ritual time and space and together engage in a bold act of imagination. We dare to appropriate the very vision of existence that Jesus inaugurated, the vision of the kingdom of God, in which all our conventional wisdom yields to the wisdom of God's mercy and grace. What we pretend is a world in which the gospel of God is truly the center of our existence.

Simultaneously, the Spirit of God is active with a commensurate agenda. Even as we human actors suspend ordinary time in favor of imagining the values of the kingdom, God does even more. God is indeed calling the kingdom of God into being, transforming the stuff of our lives by means of Word and Sacrament. The mystery of worship occurs in the interplay between these two factors: (1) our imagining the kingdom and (2) God's actual creation of the same kingdom reality. This dialectic reflects a new sort of *simul justus et peccator.* We are at the same time those who imagine and those who actually receive the kingdom of God.

Eucharistic Drama

To say that liturgy is the "work of the people" signifies something more profound than congregation members joining together to follow an order of worship. As important as it is to have the laity involved in worship— singing, praying, reading, serving—good liturgy entails another dimension, often neglected. The missing element is that of the imagination! When a worshiper gathers in the name of God, he or she covenants to suspend ordinary roles for a time in order to claim his or her ultimate identity. Worship affords the occasion to rehearse the role of one's true self, a citizen of God's kingdom.

Examine the ways in which we pretend the kingdom as we enact the eucharistic drama. By the very invocation of God's presence, we enter into " kingdom reality." We confess the truth about ourselves, that we are sinners "in thought, word, and deed" who have sinned "by what we have done and by what we have left undone." We do not enter into pretense but admit who we really are, sinful citizens of the kingdom. And we receive God's kingdom pardon with trust and gratitude for Jesus' sake.

We sing hearty kingdom songs of praise to God for all the gifts received. We demonstrate our inmost identity that we are made to glorify God. In the kingdom we implore God for mercy—for ourselves, the church, and the whole creation. And we live in the confidence that mercy and peace are exactly what God does provide. We pay attention to God's kingdom word as the central teaching of our lives. Scripture, originating among the people of God in ancient times and places, becomes again a living word for the gathered people of God today.

In the sermon, the preacher invites hearers to imagine the world of the text in such a way that the gospel makes a difference, and life is transformed into kingdom. Walter Brueggemann has helped reawaken us to the imaginative world of the Bible by which our conventional standards yield to kingdom values. The sermon summons us to surrender old grudges that make us bitter, reconcile ourselves to outlandish company, and envision a world in equity and peace. Transformation takes place in the imagining and enacting inspired by the ancient words of Scripture as interpreted by a visionary preacher.

We pledge kingdom allegiance in the words of the Apostles' or Nicene Creed. This confession is not merely on the lips but of the heart, a confession for which loyal citizens would be willing to die. We offer kingdom prayer for the whole people of God in Christ Jesus, for all people according to their needs, and for the whole creation. We withhold from God neither our own deepest needs nor those of our neighbor, but let them be known to our gracious God.

We extend a greeting of kingdom peace to one another, especially to those from whom we have become estranged. The kingdom of God is a kingdom of peace in which all are reconciled and joined together in egalitarian community. We offer the first fruits of ourselves, our time, and our possessions in gratitude for the life and blessings God has granted us. This offering is made available for the common good as a sign of the in-breaking kingdom.

New members are received by kingdom washing in the name of Christ. Young and old are incorporated into the body of Christ, under the pledge to dedicate themselves to learning Christ's way and walking in Christ's paths. This faith is affirmed and confirmed as we return time and again to the kingdom promises of grace and forgiveness first uttered by God in baptism. In response to what God has given, citizens of the kingdom commit themselves "to proclaim the good news of God in Christ through word and deed, to serve all people, following the example of Jesus, and to strive for justice and peace in all the earth."

Kingdom bread is shared around a common table. All are welcome to partake, and there is enough for all! This food satisfies not only the body's hunger but also the hunger of the heart. Jesus is present to feed with forgiveness, love, and eternal life. The entire communion of saints, believers of every past age and those from distant places, are present in the eucharistic event. Those who gather in this place are part of a universal company. All join together to pray the kingdom prayer that Jesus taught them.

Friends depart with a kingdom blessing from God. Deep within the soul, kingdom peace abides. Citizens of the kingdom move outward in lives of service to God and neighbor, remembering the poor and sharing the good news.

In the drama of the Eucharist, we imagine that we are already people of the kingdom. In standing and kneeling, singing and listening, washing and eating, praying and blessing, we immerse ourselves in the kingdom reality as envisioned by Jesus. At worship, we become parables of kingdom, imagining our lives in community as Jesus would have them. By the power of God indeed, the kingdom comes among us!

There are numerous ways in which congregational worship can be enhanced to encourage imaginative enactment of the kingdom. The very use of chant in the liturgy indicates this is a time and place set apart from all others. There is nowhere else where we interact with one another in this mode. The mood of worship is one of *epiclēsis*, invoking and imploring the Spirit of God to come and enliven us by its presence. This means interruptions to worship—announcements, applause, and all else that disturbs the atmosphere of the kingdom—should be kept to a minimum.

Silence, by contrast, serves not as an interruption but as the occasion for a potential irruption of the Spirit.

Art and architecture contribute powerfully to the ritual enactment of God's kingdom. The font deserves prominence as the entryway through which one is washed into the kingdom. The altar is a table, adorned with festive and symbolic paraments for the kingdom meal. Stained glass and vestments bespeak the alternative world one enters in worship. The architecture itself is designed to facilitate the congregational drama in which the kingdom comes.

Those who plan the worship service do well to select a prominent theme to highlight on a given Sunday. For example, today we recall that Jesus is the Good Shepherd or today we give thanks for God's gifts in baptism. Accenting a major theme, usually taken from the lectionary in relationship to the church year, lends focus to the imagination and unites all those who gather for worship. This theme can be announced at the outset and reinforced through the propers for the day. This means careful planning to highlight the day's theme in the drama, sermon, prayers, and hymns. Especially meaningful can be the use of the psalm antiphon and an invitation to communion that reinforce the central theme. As the worshipers are sent into the world, there is no question about what the congregation has imagined on a given Sunday.

The wonder of worship, however, is greater than what we imagine. We hold the faith that worship is not so much what we do but what God does in Word and Sacrament. If the best we can do is pretend, God can do something better. God takes the materials of our lives and joins them by the power of the Word to create the very kingdom for which we long. Through the word of the Gospel and the administration of the Sacraments, God activates the forgiveness, deliverance from evil, community, and eternal life that by our power we can only imagine. God produces that which we can only pretend, the real presence of Jesus Christ and his kingdom.

The mystery of worship is that God employs our eucharistic drama as means for spiritual transformation. Regular and frequent worship becomes an imperative for those who would live as citizens of the kingdom. To pray "Thy kingdom come" entails commitment to dedicated rehearsal of one's role. "Practice makes perfect," as they say. As we gather for worship to pretend the kingdom, we gradually find ourselves transformed. Individually, Christ is really present to meet our spiritual needs for forgiveness, hope, and wholeness. Corporately, we discover ourselves being shaped into the body of Christ. God is as alive among us now as in ancient times and places!

"Go in Peace; Serve the Lord"

The most important thing a congregation does is gather for worship: *Worship is the single most important factor in forming Christian identity.* Moreover, worship mediates the energy that transforms congregations into centers for mission. As one moves from worship in the sanctuary into the routines of daily life, it is as though one were crossing the border into another land. Our baptism serves as our passport, validating our identity as citizens of the kingdom. Participation in the eucharistic drama issues us a visa that enables our travel in a foreign country.

The concluding exhortation of worship, "go in peace; serve the Lord," calls to mind the *paraenesis* so integral to the Pauline epistles. There lives a dynamic interplay between what takes place at worship and the "liturgy" of daily life. The Christian faith is not something exclusively reserved for Sunday mornings. Nor can it be contained in proper forms, either liturgical or doctrinal. Rather, Christian faith is to be lived out in the daily ministry of all the baptized.

At worship we rehearse life in the kingdom of God. Here one discovers the true self. Among the selves that compete for priority in the human psyche, there exists a self made in the image of Christ. Forgiven, compassionate, and hope-filled, this true self is given shape and nurtured in the experience of Christian liturgy. Nowhere do we feel more at home, more the person God intends us to be, than at worship. Our inmost identity is that of a baptized child of God. We express our true self in confession, absolution, glorifying God, attending to God's word, offering first fruits to God's service, and partaking of Christ at the holy table.

Similarly, it is at worship that we discover the true nature of human community. Humanity is created by God to live together as family. All are brothers and sisters with God as nurturing, mentoring parent. In imagining God's kingdom through the liturgy, we relate to God and one another honestly, freely, and in mutual acceptance. We experience the truth that all are welcome. We find our own gifts affirmed as necessary for the well-being of the body of Christ.

These discoveries about ourselves, God, and the nature of community transform our lives. By our participation in the alternative world of worship, our values and priorities change. Eventually, we may discover that we are no longer sure what it means to speak of the "real" world. Is the world of ordinary work, family, and routine the "real" world? Or is perhaps the world of worship, the enactment of the kingdom, in a more profound sense the "real" world? Which of these worlds has deeper significance for the ordering of my life? Which of these worlds partakes of eternity and will last forever? We may discover that one day we find ourselves believing that the world of the kingdom as imagined in worship is the most real of all.

The life of every congregation unfolds in the dynamic relationship between identity formation and the movement into mission. Both elements are integral to wholesome congregational life. Both are rooted deeply in the liturgy. Evangelizing, global connections, ecumenism, and social ministry each finds its grounding in the kingdom imagined and brought into being in the world of worship.

The impetus to change the world, which is provoked by worship, arises from the dissonance between the values of the conventional world and those of the kingdom of God. The early church acquired a reputation as those who "turned the world upside down" (Acts 17:6). Conventional values concerning family, wealth, honor, and religion, each is subverted by the wisdom of Jesus—the kingdom and the cross. In this process, two dangers can arise: (1) the dissonance is so great as to undermine any serious hope for changing the world or (2) the church domesticates the volatile wisdom of Jesus. In spite of these distortions, an impulse to world transformation permeates the liturgy.

On an individual scale, I desire to become reconciled with those from whom I am estranged. If God has forgiven me so much and demonstrated infinite mercy by the death of Christ on the cross, how can I withhold forgiveness from those who have offended me? To deny pardon to one's debtors is to negate the full mercy of Christ and opt instead for resentment as the ultimate reality. Where conventional wisdom counsels an eye for an eye, the unconventional wisdom of Jesus moves Christian people to forgive as they have been forgiven.

Whereas every individual longs for direction in life, the word of God, read and interpreted at worship, lends orientation and guidance. As contemporary lives are juxtaposed with the lives of biblical characters, discoveries are made about the reality of God's grace, prompting new responses to life's challenges. Destructive patterns are unmasked as we witness the foibles of ancient sinners whose motives and behavior are as compromised as our own. Yet the overriding message is that of God's mercy, love, and grace, sufficient to amend and redirect even the likes of them—and us. Individual persons receive hope and new perspective from the living Word.

As the gospel is proclaimed, sung, prayed, sprinkled, and eaten, an awareness dawns: there is no message like this on earth. The impulse to evangelizing also is deeply rooted in worship. Like other types of good news, this best news demands to be shared. There are countless lives that would be enhanced and saved if only this gospel were known and received. Worshipers who experience the gospel of the kingdom and cross are transformed into agents of the *kerygma*. Worship makes evangelists of us, eager to share what we have found.

The prayers of the church foster compassion for the sick, the grieving, the battered, the homeless, and for all God's afflicted creatures near at hand. Through the rituals of peace, one is impelled to live as a representative of peace wherever conflict threatens the common good. The offering and shared eucharistic bread instill the sense that everything we have is a gift from God to be shared generously with those in need.

On a corporate scale, worship activates social ministry. Not everyone will agree about what this means in practice. Many will recognize that the eucharistic drama includes the relief of human suffering from the effects of disasters, famine, and war. Such deeds of charity are a direct consequence of imagining the world as the kingdom of God at worship.

Some will further organize to undertake the excruciating task of transforming the structures of society according to the promises of the kingdom. This requires engagement in political movements for change and stirs up controversy about the appropriate relationship between church and state. While it is possible to differ regarding strategies and plans of action, the fundamental impulse to change the world is an authentic consequence of participation in Christian liturgy. The level of frustration experienced by those who carry kingdom values into efforts for social change necessitates both frequent return to liturgical celebration and a healthy sense of humor, as one recognizes the incongruity between the way things are and the way God intends them to be.

Finally, the liturgy moves us to reclaim the unity of the church. As we confess our faith in one, holy, catholic, and apostolic church, we are reminded of the current dismemberment of Christ's body into competing and often antagonistic factions. As in worship, we imagine a "united kingdom," we anticipate the reconciliation of all Christians through dialogue, cooperation, and shared worship. Furthermore, we are reminded that Christian fellowship extends beyond national borders and unites peoples of every race, language, and tribe.

By our participation in worship, we receive not only our identity but our mission. The remainder of this book develops the themes introduced in this chapter. The theology of the congregation here envisioned—both identity and mission—begins with the divine worship of God by the people in the congregation.

FOR FURTHER READING

Bell, Catherine. *Ritual Theory, Ritual Practice.* Oxford: Oxford University Press, 1992.

Driver, Tom F. *The Magic of Ritual: Our Need for Liberating Rites that Transform Our Lives and Our Communities.* San Francisco: HarperSanFrancisco, 1991.

Kavanagh, Aidan. *On Liturgical Theology.* Collegeville, Minn.: Liturgical, 1984.

Lathrop, Gordon W. *Central Things: Worship in Word and Sacrament*. Minneapolis: Augsburg Fortress, 2005.

Pfatteicher, Philip H. *The School of the Church: Worship and Christian Formation*. Valley Forge, Pa.: Trinity Press International, 1995.

Saliers, Don E. *Worship as Theology: Foretaste of Glory Divine*. Nashville: Abingdon, 1994.

Schattauer, Thomas H. *Inside Out: Worship in an Age of Mission*. Minneapolis: Fortress Press, 1999.

Schmemann, Alexander. *Introduction to Liturgical Theology*. Translated by Asheleigh E. Moorhouse. Crestwood, N.Y.: St. Vladimir's Seminary Press, 1997.

Turner, Victor, Roger Abrahams, and Alfred Harris. *The Ritual Process: Structure and Anti-Structure*. Chicago: Aldine Transaction, 1995.

Wells, Samuel. *Improvisation: The Drama of Christian Ethics*. Grand Rapids: Brazos, 2004.

Wengert, Timothy J., and Gordon W. Lathrop. *Christian Assembly: Marks of the Church in a Pluralistic Age*. Minneapolis: Fortress Press, 2004.

White, James F. *Introduction to Christian Worship*. Third Edition. Nashville: Abingdon, 2001.

FOR REFLECTION AND DISCUSSION

1. When have you had the experience of an "alternative world"? What effect did that experience have on your life?

2. How does imagination affect life? What influence has your imagination had on the course of your life?

3. Reflect on the difference worship has made in your life. Have you ever had a transformative experience as a worshiper? If so, explain what that means to you.

4. What parts of the liturgy have had the most profound influence on your life? Describe what difference they have made on you.

5. What is the connection between liturgical worship and the "real" world? How are you a different person in the rest of your life because you have worshiped God?

PART TWO: IDENTITY

INTRODUCTION

How do you answer the question about who you are? The answers we choose to employ tell much about how we perceive our own identity. After the sharing of your name, do you choose to refer to the members of your family or to what you do for a living? Do you talk about your hobbies or where you live? Do you ever get around to mentioning the fact that you are baptized or that you belong to a particular congregation?

The question about identity goes to the core of our personhood. It aims to uncover the essence of our humanity. In a parallel way, the identity of a congregation is disclosed by the particular way it organizes and conducts its essential life together. After you tell someone the name of your congregation, what are the next characteristics that you would name to disclose the essence of its identity?

In part 2, we explore four basic themes of congregational life that especially serve the formation of congregational identity: prayer, education, life in community, and stewardship. Each of these functions also has direct implications for mission. But they first build up fundamental congregational identity on the way to leading the congregation into outreach.

Prayer connects the congregation to the life of God, whether the praying takes place at worship, in small groups, or in personal devotions. In intercessory prayer, we join our petitions to the prayers of Jesus Christ for the sake of the needs of the church and the world. When prayer permeates the work of the congregation, God draws near.

In this post-Christian age, the educational efforts of the congregation become more important than ever. Christian faith competes with many other priorities and commitments in the lives of the baptized. Our educational ministry in such a post-Christian era needs to involve intentional focus on making disciples of Jesus. What does it mean to follow Jesus, not only when we are present in the church building but in every time, place, and activity?

Life in community for the members of a congregation means living together under the cross. We trust Christ's promise that he is present wherever two or three are gathered in his name. Moreover, we dare to believe that Christ manifests a particular presence as we encounter him among the poor, oppressed, and abandoned. The church discovers the living presence of Christ as it ministers to the least of these, Christ's sisters and brothers in their need.

Stewardship involves the bold confession that God is the owner of all things; we are but the caretakers accountable to God for how we manage what has been placed in our service. Tithing can be a vital spiritual discipline as we seek to acknowledge God as the giver of all good gifts, including life itself. We offer thanks to God by extending the circle of care to encompass all of creation.

Together, these themes contribute to a lively sense of congregational identity, reminding us *whose we are* and preparing us to move out in mission to the community and world. As we reclaim God's presence at the core of our life together, God sets us free for service to our neighbors by the power of the gospel of Jesus Christ.

Chapter Five

Prayer: Your Kingdom Come!

If God is alive as the One who brings the kingdom into the world and our midst, prayer functions as essential communication between God and God's people. The congregation as a spiritual organization depends for its life on the real presence of the living God in its midst. In a world that continues to succumb to the increasing pressures of secularization and despair, living faith in God cannot be taken for granted. John Westerhoff once posed the pointed question: "Will our children have faith?" The church has always depended upon the transmission of the Christian faith from generation to generation. Today, many children are not following in the footsteps of their parents' faith. To revisit Westerhoff's question by adding a poignant twist, we might ask: Will our faith have children? In other words, will our faith be vibrant enough to be transmitted to the generation that follows us? The answer to this question depends in no small measure on whether we learn and teach others to live in prayerful relationship with their God.

Congregations that participate in the inventory process based on Christian Schwarz's book *Natural Church Development* have used that instrument to explore what they are doing well in ministry and where they need to grow. Almost predictably, congregations in mainline denominations discover their weakest area in what Schwarz calls "passionate spirituality." Passionate spirituality involves vivid expectancy about God's participation in human life. It involves spiritual awareness of God's hand at work in daily affairs. It involves perception of God's face in the faces of other people. It involves the conviction that God is actively present in the actual lives of people in the world today, beginning with one's local congregation.

The key to reviving passionate spirituality among God's people is an active life of prayer, taught and caught in the life of the congregation. The prayer life of a congregation encompasses several dimensions, three of which receive focused attention in this chapter: the role of the pastor in leading the congregation in praying, the place of intercessory prayer in the worshiping assembly, and the importance of teaching God's people, young and old, how to pray.

Leading the People of God in Prayer

The leader of a spiritual community (such as a congregation) must be continually replenished in his/her own spiritual life. How can a spiritual leader be a shepherd who nourishes the members of the flock when malnourished her/himself? The work of the pastor is demanding. Schedules are overfull. Emotions often run high. Conflicts take their toll on one's well-being. Many distractions emerge. The pressure of the immediate can easily overtake the focus on what's necessary. A life of prayer is one of the central things which always remains necessary.

Too often when we speak about the prayer life of the pastor, we think of a narrow set of practices as a "one size fits all" prescription. For this reason we can be thankful at the recent recognition and affirmation that there are many different types of spirituality and forms of prayer that nourish people differently, depending on personality.

Employing an inventory based on the Myers-Briggs Type Indicator, Sandra Krebs Hirsch and Jane Kise, in their book, *Soultypes: Matching Your Personality and Spiritual Path,* have developed an eightfold typology for understanding the nature of one's own spiritual hunger. The eight different spiritual paths are organized according to the four categories of the Myers-Briggs Type Indicator: sensing, intuition, thinking, or feeling. The sensing- and intuition-based spiritual paths include (1) extraverted sensing: the active spiritual path, (2) introverted sensing: the time-honored spiritual path, (3) extraverted intuition: the catalytic spiritual path, and (4) introverted intuition: the illuminating spiritual path. The thinking- and feeling-based spiritual paths include (5) extraverted thinking: the analytical spiritual path, (6) introverted thinking: the conceptual spiritual path, (7) extraverted feeling: the community-oriented spiritual path, and (8) introverted feeling: the personal spiritual path.

Even this brief introduction to the variety of spiritualities (and thereby also forms of prayer) provides direction for the pastor and spiritual leader to imagine and explore a range of spiritual practices, according to one's own proclivities. Not only may one consider the conventional practices of following a devotional book and individual Bible reading, but rather an extensive set of classical and innovative spiritual practices deserve consideration: walking meditation, praying the hours, artistic creation, contemplative prayer, meditative study, journaling, spiritual direction, centering prayer, *lectio divina*, walking a labyrinth, intercessory prayer, and a host of other possibilities. A vast library of resources is available for investigating and implementing these spiritual practices.

The crucial factor is renewal of the soul, in order that the leader is replenished with spiritual energy for leading the people of God in their own search for identity and mission. The adeptness of the pastor in spiritual practices becomes in turn a resource for accompanying others in their spiritual lives.

One of the privileges afforded the pastor as a spiritual leader is the invitation to lead corporate prayer. The occasions when a pastor is called upon to pray are manifold and diverse. Not only may the pastor be called upon to pray at the different functions within the congregation but also in public settings, like a city council meeting or baccalaureate service. How does one think theologically about the purpose of prayer on such occasions?

First, it is always crucial to discern the particularities of the context. Who are the people gathered together at this time and place? Who are those noticeably absent from the gathering who also need to be encompassed by the prayer? Do all those present share the Christian faith? What are these people thinking and feeling at this moment? What ought they be thinking and feeling? How do you imagine the longings of the human heart here and now? What is the larger context of this occasion? Where did we come from and where are we going? What is unique about this moment in history? How does the larger culture and global situation affect those who are gathered? Where does this occasion fit into the larger scheme of God's story over time? To apprehend the complex dimensions of the particular context, it may be very suitable to begin the prayer with silence, in order to gather all thoughts together in the moment.

Second, prayer serves to align the lives of the people gathered together with the larger purposes of God in bringing forth the kingdom. By virtue of the fact that we are praying, we are calling upon God to be present and act in our lives. God's purposes are always for salvation and wholeness. This means the prayers we utter appeal to the reality of God as has been revealed in God's pattern of mercy and faithfulness in Jesus Christ. Whether we name the name of Jesus in our prayer is not the most important issue. There are certain public occasions where one might choose to pray in the name of the Creator or in the name of the Spirit, depending on the makeup of the assembly. More important, however, is that there emerges an alignment of the gathered community with the kingdom purposes of God. Among God's kingdom purposes are forgiveness, reconciliation, healing, deliverance from evil, sufficiency in the basic necessities of life, justice, peace, love, and hope. These are among the gifts that God seeks to bestow upon us.

In public prayer, we aim to articulate honestly the needs of the gathered community and to connect these needs with the kingdom which God seeks to inaugurate among us. The degree to which the prayer honestly names the genuine needs of the people conditions how God's kingdom becomes manifest to those with the eyes to see and the ears to hear. A prayer that fails to apprehend the deep needs of the gathered assembly is a weak vehicle for the in-breaking of God's merciful and healing presence. By contrast, a prayer which captures honestly and boldly the human condition allows the reality of God to enter unobstructed into human affairs with power and abundance of grace. Leading corporate prayer is a

charism closely related to truth telling. Public prayer aims at an alignment of genuine human hopes and tragedies with the reality of the God
who promises the kingdom.

Reflecting on the responsibility for leading public prayer from
another angle, the task is that of invoking the presence of God in the
moment and creating expectancy among others that God's presence makes
a difference.

Let us consider again the power of Jesus' parables. Jesus was a story-
teller, but the stories he told were of a very particular genre. The parables are all stories taken from the commonplace settings in daily life, not
unlike the stuff of our own daily existence. Yet these commonplace settings become the arena for extraordinary interventions when God enters
the scene. Estrangement between a father and his children becomes the
occasion for unimaginable mercy (Prodigal Son). Happening upon an
accident victim becomes the occasion for inexplicable generosity (Good
Samaritan). Seedtime and harvest become the occasion for discovering
God's reckless agriculture (The Sower). In every instance divine presence
totally alters the expected course of events.

Those who lead the people of God in prayer have the awesome responsibility of so invoking God's name that people arrive at a new expectancy
that God's presence is real and God's intervention will make all the difference. While we may live in a world of disenchantment (Charles Taylor),
where faith in God's activity has ebbed, the act of prayer counters the
tide of unbelief with the expectation that God is alive and still reign-
ing. Whether at worship or in the classroom, whether at a funeral home
or wedding celebration, whether in a park or at a community event, the
pastor leads the people in prayer with the expectation that God makes a
difference and will deliver on God's promises.

Let Us Pray for . . .

"With the whole people of God in Christ Jesus, let us pray for the church,
those in need, and all of God's creation." Central to Christian worship and
to the life of Christian prayer are the intercessions. Intercessory prayer
involves asking or beseeching God to intervene in the life of the world

in some way. Intercessory prayer is prayer *for* someone or something. At worship, we invite the gathered congregation to join together in relating to God around core concerns. The primary purpose of the intercessions is less praying for ourselves and much more about bringing the needs of others before the presence of Almighty God.

The central theological idea in intercessory prayer is that the assembly joins the prayer of Jesus Christ, who intercedes for the needs of the world. Jesus Christ is the one mediator between human beings and God. Thomas Schattauer teaches: "Remember that Christ voices his own intercession for the world through our prayer as an assembly of those gathered in him. The prayers of intercession are first of all Christ's own prayer for the world, not simply our prayers." This is a profound understanding of what takes place when the church offers intercessions on behalf of others. In a sense, the church in intercessory prayer seeks to align its concern for the world with God's own concern.

The living Christ in his earthly ministry did not only enter into prayer for the needs of others. Rather, it is the conviction of the church that the crucified and risen Christ continues to live and continues to offer to God prayers which articulate exactly what the world needs. This is what it means to pray in the name of Jesus Christ. Christ is the mediator, and we join our prayers to his own prayer of intercession.

The expression of the particular needs of individuals, groups, or the creation itself belongs to this larger context of Christ's prayer for the world. In intercessory prayer the church brings to expression all the world's needs in the presence of God. We are mindful of God's agenda in and for the world, which Jesus called the coming of the kingdom. Intercessory prayer challenges the people to transcend private concern for their own welfare and to place their own needs in the larger context of the needs of others and the needs of the entire world. Walter Huffman writes: "To pray the world to God—remembering the needs of the hungry, poor, the dying, nations at war, societies in disarray, nature contaminated by waste—is to sense something of our solidarity with God's creation and with those for whom Christ died."

Often, intercessory prayer is narrowed by self-concern. When we begin to pray, we think first and primarily of what we need for ourselves.

While this is a natural impulse and also appropriate in devotional prayers, intercessory prayer invites us to conversion—to turn from self and see the enormity of the needs of the world, all of which are of deep concern to our God. To carry forward such an agenda requires thoughtful stewardship in the preparation of the intercessions.

In many traditions, the pastor serves as the primary steward of the congregation's prayer life, including the formulation of the congregation's intercessions. Increasingly, however, the intercessions are becoming the work of the assisting minister, who also leads the congregation in offering these prayers. While there are many aids to intercessory prayer available in worship resources or books of prayer, the crafting of the intercessions as they are prayed in a particular congregation at a particular time deserves thoughtful attention. How do we articulate the needs of the world in such a way that the needs of this congregation come to profound expression? Those charged with responsibility for the intercessions need to take the time necessary to create beautiful and animated prayers that capture the significance of what Christ prays for us and for the world. This responsibility is no less important than the preparation of the sermon itself.

As suggested in the last chapter, a worship committee may play a wonderful role in contributing to the design not only the shape of the liturgy but the shape of the congregation's intercessions on a given Sunday. The season of the church year and the lectionary texts can provide images and themes to draw together the prayers of the church with the rest of the service. While the responsibility for the writing of the prayers may fall to the assisting minister in partnership with the pastor, listening carefully to the insights of others in the congregation helps to expand the meaning of the intercessions as the prayer of the people. A book such as Huffman's *Prayer of the Faithful: Understanding and Creatively Leading Corporate Intercessory Prayer* can provide constructive guidance in the creative process.

As a guide for considering the range of concerns brought forward to God by the congregation at worship (particularly on Sunday), there are classical categories for preparing the intercessions. Traditionally, these seven categories have been followed in a standard order.

First, there is prayer for the church universal, its ministry, and the mission of the gospel. We are drawn in the intercessions out of our tendency toward parochialism and claim our place in the one, holy, catholic, apostolic church. We are reminded that the church as a whole has a ministry of which our congregation is but one part. We are summoned to pray for the mission of the gospel in the world. This is Christ's great mission of bringing forth the kingdom. Note how this first category of intercession grounds us fundamentally in our identity and mission as a congregation.

Second, we pray for the well-being of creation. For too long the church has neglected this concern as part of its calling! Over the centuries, the church has taken creation for granted as merely a means to be used for human benefit rather than seeing creation as having its own intrinsic value in being deemed "good" by the Creator. As the environment faces crisis due to human excess, intercessions for the well-being of creation take on a new urgency.

Third, there is prayer for peace and justice in the world, the nations and those in authority, the community, and those who govern. We read in the newspaper and hear on news reports the devastation facing multitudes of people due to violence and injustice. In the intercessions, we name these people and situations which are of concern to God in Christ and make them our own concern. Moreover, we pray for those in positions of authority to govern with integrity and with special regard for the weakest and most vulnerable people.

Fourth, we pray for the poor, oppressed, the sick, the bereaved, the lonely, and all who suffer in body, mind, or spirit. A theology of the cross undergirds the prayers of intercession. Because the crucified Christ extends particular compassion to those who suffer in any way, so also the church consistently holds up the needs of the suffering in its prayers.

Fifth, there is prayer for the congregation and for special concerns. At this place, the congregation raises its own concerns and joins them to the prayer of Christ for the world. It is fitting and proper that the needs of the congregation, including any special concerns, be articulated as part of the intercessions. But these concerns take their place alongside all the pressing needs of others which have already come to voice.

Sixth, we may include additional prayers from the assembly. This can be a moving and vital dimension of the intercessions. It can be structured in several different ways. The pastor or assisting minister may have gathered these concerns prior to the service in a book or orally. Or the people may be invited to speak aloud their intercessions, either successively or en masse. In any case, this form of intercession contributes much to making the intercessions truly the prayers of the people as the assembly joins its inmost fears and hopes to the prayer of Christ.

Seventh, there is prayer for the faithful departed, including those who have recently died and those commemorated on the church calendar. We are part of a church that includes the living and the dead, saints whom we remember as an inspiration for the church's own faith journey and saints whom we have known in the living of our own lives. To pray for the faithful departed places the intercessions in the context of our own finitude. And we are regularly reminded by this intercession of the promise of eternal life that belongs both to us and to those for whom we pray.

"Into your hands, gracious God, we commend all for whom we pray, trusting in your mercy; through Jesus Christ, our Savior." Thus concludes the intercessory prayer. Finally, God is the one to whom we entrust all of our prayers. For Christ's sake, we dare to believe that God embraces our prayer as the prayer of God's own dear Son.

While the form of intercessory prayer avoids personal agendas and jeremiads that push private causes, it is nevertheless the case that as we join our prayer to the prayer of Christ, that for which we pray becomes core to the very mission priorities of the congregation. Intercessory prayer does establish certain values and commitments which guide the congregation in its ministry and mission. If we pray for those affected by violence, victims of hurricanes, the hungry, the sick, or the grieving, how can these also not become the persons for whom we engage ourselves in our daily vocations and congregational outreach? In this way, we become what we pray!

Lord, Teach Us to Pray!

Where did you learn to pray? My earliest memories of prayer are from my Sunday school class when I was three years old and from the bedtime prayers at home. I can still recite the prayers we prayed when I was a child. No one actually taught me how to pray. But my parents and god-parents took the time to practice prayer with me.

I would surmise that my own experience would be similar to many others. No one actually taught us how to pray. Rather, we learned this basic Christian activity as it was modeled for us by parents or other significant adults. In this way, prayer was learned, like so much else in life, not through instruction but through a process of socialization into how one leads one's life.

This pattern of learning prayer from one's parents and family may be endangered in this generation. In many homes, the demands of work have meant the fragmentation of family life, so that parents have not modeled prayer for their children. In fact, many of those who are now parents may not have ever had prayer modeled for them. All of this means a new responsibility has emerged for the church in the last generations: teaching people how to pray.

We cannot assume that young people or their parents know how to pray, even though they may participate regularly in congregational worship services. Listening to worship leaders pray is not the same as knowing how to pray oneself. For this reason, alongside the other forms of instruction which the church has begun to regularize for young people (Bible reading or first Communion preparation), the congregation does well to initiate a curriculum designed to teach young people to pray. Perhaps the best instruction in this regard would be classes or workshops where children attend with their parents. Part of the instruction can be giving assignments where parents begin actually to pray with their children.

The church is in the situation today, however, where not only children need to be taught how to pray. Adults, both longtime and new members, need to be taught the basics of Christian prayer and its importance in the life of faith. In such instruction, learners can discover both the variety of prayer types and can practice praying alone or with others in a safe environment. One of the greatest blessings of such a class is experiencing the joy and satisfaction of praying together with other people of faith, either in a trusted small group or even with a single prayer partner. Such exercise in learning to pray can have a ripple effect in strengthening other congregational ministries, from small groups to committee meetings.

As the people of God learn to pray, they can explore the rich variety in forms of praying and types of prayer. There are several distinctive forms for praying, some already having been named in this chapter: walking prayer, praying the labyrinth, centering prayer, contemplative prayer, devotional prayer, reading prayer, working prayer, singing prayer, or liturgical prayer. The classical types of prayer include: adoration, praise, confession (or expiation), healing, meditation, intercession (also supplication or petition) and thanksgiving. One of the most popular acronyms for remembering a variety of types of prayer is A.C.T.S.: adoration, confession, thanksgiving, and supplication.

The disciples came to Jesus in the New Testament and asked him: "Lord, teach us to pray. . . ." (Luke 11:1-4). In response, Jesus taught them the prayer we know today as the Lord's Prayer. The Lord's Prayer remains the treasure of Christian prayer to this day. This prayer contains the essence of what we need to pray for in concentrated petitions. For this reason, the church continues to teach the meaning of the Lord's Prayer in its catechesis from generation to generation. Like the disciples, the people in our congregations need to be taught how to pray. The Lord's Prayer is the paradigmatic prayer that guides our instruction. Children at an early age and adults at every stage of life can benefit from instruction in how to pray to God, building on the prayer Jesus taught his disciples: "Our Father in heaven . . ."

FOR FURTHER READING

Finck, Murray D. *Stretch and Pray: A Daily Discipline for Physical and Spiritual Wellness.* Minneapolis: Augsburg Books, 2005.

Foster, Richard J. *Prayer: Finding the Heart's True Home.* San Francisco: HarperSanFrancisco, 1992.

Hirsh, Sandra Krebs and Jane A. G. Kise. *Soultypes: Matching Your Personality and Spiritual Path.* Minneapolis: Augsburg Fortress, 2006.

Huffman, Walter C. *Prayer of the Faithful: Understanding and Creatively Leading Corporate Intercessory Prayer.* Minneapolis: Augsburg Fortress, 1992.

Johnson, Maxwell E. *Benedictine Daily Prayer: A Short Breviary.* Collegeville, Minn.: Liturgical, 2005.

Jungmann, Joseph A. *Christian Prayer Through the Centuries.* Revised Edition. Edited by Christopher Irving. Mahwah, N.J.: Paulist, 2008.

Lathrop, Gordon W. *The Pastor: A Spirituality.* Minneapolis: Fortress Press, 2006.

Nouwen, Henri. *Life of the Beloved: Spiritual Living in a Secular World.* Tenth Anniversary Edition. New York: Crossroad, 2002.

Simon, Arthur. *Rediscovering the Lord's Prayer.* Minneapolis: Augsburg, 2005.

Thompson, Marjorie J. *Soul Feast: An Invitation to the Christian Spiritual Life.* Louisville: Westminster John Knox, 2005.

Underhill, Evelyn. *Essential Writings.* Maryknoll, N.Y.: Orbis, 2003.

Westerhoff, John H. *Will Our Children Have Faith?* Revised Edition. New York: Morehouse, 2000.

FOR REFLECTION AND DISCUSSION

1. What does "passionate spirituality" mean to you? Can you give examples of passionate spirituality in the life of your congregation?

2. Which forms of praying come most naturally to you? Which forms are difficult? How can you affirm the uniqueness of your own spirituality type?

3. What do you appreciate most about intercessory prayer? What difference do the intercessions make in the life of your congregation?

4. How did you learn to pray? What are the most important insights that you have learned about prayer as you have grown in faith?

5. When did you learn the Lord's Prayer? What importance does the Lord's Prayer have in your life and in the life of your congregation?

Chapter Six

Education:
Making Disciples

Prior to the baptism of children, parents and sponsors promise to bring the baptized faithfully to worship; to teach them the Lord's Prayer, Creed, and Ten Commandments; to place in their hands the holy Scriptures; and to provide for their instruction in the Christian faith. The object of these promises is to ensure that the baptized live in the covenant of their baptism and in communion with the church and lead godly lives until the day of Jesus Christ. Such promises are easily spoken by those presenting a candidate for baptism. Yet the fulfillment of these promises too often falls by the wayside.

This chapter argues that the chief educational priority of the Christian church in our time is the fulfillment of the baptismal charge: "to make disciples of all nations." The risen Jesus Christ left this great commission for the church: "Go therefore and make disciples of all nations, baptizing them in the name of the Father and of the Son and of the Holy Spirit, and teaching them to obey everything that I have commanded you" (Matt 28:19-20). While the church over the centuries has been relatively successful with the baptizing charge of this commission, the making of disciples and teaching dimensions have been too often left to happenstance.

Responsibility for initiation into Christian belief and practice falls not exclusively to parents but to the entire Christian congregation.

As we undertake the task of Christian education in this generation, there are significant lessons to be learned from the catechetical instruction as practiced in the early centuries of the church. We need to recover the mystery of incorporation into the body of Christ which was once practiced as an arcane discipline. Like those early Christian generations, we need the model of saints and martyrs who witness to us the cost of Christian discipleship. And we need to focus on how Christian people connect their faith with ministry in daily life. In other words, we need once again to take seriously the Reformation slogan that the church is "the priesthood of all believers."

Arcane Discipline

For more than fifteen hundred years, one could presume that Western civilization was based on Christian foundations. The era of Christendom commenced during the fourth century, when Constantine and subsequent Roman emperors gave favored status to the Christian faith. The close alliance of church and state found its apex in the medieval church. Being a Christian became virtually indistinguishable from being a citizen. The church functioned as a broker of power alongside and frequently in competition with the state. Though much changed with the modern world and the emergence of the nation-state as the primary arbiter of political power, Christianity continued to provide the religious fiber holding Western society together.

In recent history, however, there is a cacophony of voices declaring that the age of Christendom has come to an end. Not only is our age described as postmodern but also post-Christian. This means that one can no longer assume that Christianity serves as the common denominator binding together Western culture. This analysis of the present moment of history is held not only by agnostic intellectuals but by one of the foremost interpreters of the contemporary Christian church, Loren Mead.

In *The Once and Future Church*, Mead gave expression to his insightful understanding of the dilemma facing the contemporary church. In short, we are presently experiencing the collapse of the "Christendom paradigm" of the church. According to this paradigm, the church lived in close identification with the surrounding culture; being Christian was equated with being a good citizen to a large degree. The congregation saw itself as a parish, "taking care" of the membership that lived in its precinct. Mission was something that happened in distant places among foreign people.

Mead contends that many of the struggles now facing the church result from the dissolution of the presuppositions of Christendom. Even if it once were true, no longer can one dare to assume that everyone is a Christian. Nor can one assume that civic society is a direct expression of Christian values. This, in turn, means that mission is not merely a task undertaken in distant places by trained missionaries but rather something that is an imperative close to home. If we are living now in the age of post-Christendom, this means that the church in the United States must also claim its calling as a missionary church.

The crisis of the church is that we are already experiencing the multiple consequences of this new post-Christendom situation yet do not know how to proceed in a way that meets the immediate challenge. Mead also sketches in outline an earlier model, that of the pre-Constantinian church, which he calls the "apostolic paradigm." According to this paradigm, Christians belonged to the church on the basis of personal conviction and commitment, not by virtue of birth in a particular territory. The boundary existing between church and culture was well-defined. One took a deliberate and risky stance to enter and join the Christian fellowship. Often the prevailing culture lived in antagonism to the church, expressing its hostility through acts of persecution.

This chapter contends that in our current situation we have much to learn from the early church, Mead's "apostolic paradigm," in terms of Christian education. Though the corpse of Christendom remains visible, its substance is in the process of decomposing. Evidence of this dilemma is available from several quarters. One of the studies most pertinent to this theme was undertaken by the Search Institute under the title "Effective Christian Education: A National Study of Protestant Congregations." The conclusions of this study demonstrate how the inner substance of the Christian faith within the church is dissolving.

The Search Institute study measured maturity of faith according to two criteria: a horizontal component of devotion to serving the neighbor and a vertical component characterized by a deep and personal relationship to God. Among adults in the Protestant denominations studied, most registered a lack of mature faith according to this standard. An even larger number of adolescents demonstrated what the study calls "undeveloped faith." While there appeared to be a direct correlation between aging and an increasingly developed faith outlook, another factor emerged as especially significant in contributing to faith maturity: *participation in Christian education!* The single most important thing a congregation can do to promote faith development is to provide effective Christian education programming.

Christian education must be seen and understood as a lifelong undertaking. This must not simply be mouthed as an ideal but be put into practice, with adults setting the standard for the youth. The quantity of educational programs is not as important as the *quality* of the programs that are offered. A congregation is better served to develop excellence in leadership and content in its educational programs rather than providing numerous offerings shallow in quality. A surprising finding in the Search study was the crucial importance of the faith maturity of the teacher. Participants advance most significantly in their own faith development under the direction of a teacher who demonstrates highly developed faith.

At no time in the church's history did it devote more deliberate attention to Christian education than in the first three centuries. Catechesis took place in a lengthy process leading to baptism during the Easter vigil. Catechumens only gradually were initiated into the mysteries of the Christian faith. For example, those preparing for baptism might be allowed to come to worship to hear the Scripture and sermon, but they were dismissed prior to the celebration of the Eucharist. Participation in the mystery of the Eucharist was something for which one had to be carefully seasoned. The intensive catechetical process might last as long as three years with converts gradually nurtured into ever deeper understandings of Christian truth and practice.

During the struggle against the Nazi threat to the church, Dietrich Bonhoeffer sparked renewed interest in the relevance of a *disciplina arcana* (literally, "secret discipline"), making fascinating references in his *Letters and Papers from Prison*. Isolated from traditional forms of Christian community, Bonhoeffer speculated about a "religionless" Christianity in a "world come of age." Already Bonhoeffer anticipated the end of Christendom during the persecution of the church in Nazi Germany. While the church, practicing arcane discipline, would not (or could not) perform cultic or ritual acts in public (since it was fully integrated into worldly service), privately there would remain a "secret discipline," by which the church would need to reconstitute its Christian identity. By means of an arcane discipline initiating them into the way of discipleship, Christians attain maturity of faith and become prepared to live out their faith in the public, non-Christian world.

The contemporary church urgently needs a recovery of the *sense of otherness* of the Christian faith as evoked through the practice of an arcane discipline. The Christian faith is not a subject easily mastered, certainly not by adolescent confirmands or even their middle-aged parents. To believe and to live as a Christian is counterculturally distinctive from the conventional values and lifestyles of the surrounding culture. The journey into Christian discipleship is a lifelong endeavor. There are ever new mysteries and nuances of the faith to explore. In approaching Christian education, we must retrieve a sense of the wonder at the depths of Christian wisdom, which presents a challenge to all ages for discovering new dimensions and implications of the Christian mystery.

Three words summarize the goals of an effective congregational Christian education program: to *learn*, to *think,* and to *live* the Christian story. In everything a congregation does, the awareness should prevail that being Christian is something unique and distinctive. For those familiar with the work of James W. Fowler, these three goals—learning, thinking, and living the story—can be correlated with the six stages of faith that he has articulated. Fowler argues that one's understanding of faith develops in formal stages that are related to human cognitive and psychosocial development. One proceeds in faith development through consecutive stages, not being able to bypass any given stage, but certainly capable of becoming fixed at a certain stage, which is never surpassed. While Fowler identifies six formal stages, we here focus on three educational goals.

The first task of Christian education is to assist children and members *to learn the Christian story*. This means a strong emphasis on learning Bible stories in preschool and the elementary years, with only secondary attention given to explanation of what stories mean. Music and art are marvelous media for effectively reinforcing basic Bible content. Not just a few stories but the entire biblical narrative should become familiar, even those stories from which we think children initially ought to be sheltered. It is during the elementary years that basic knowledge of the catechism should also be introduced; perhaps each school year focusing on a specific section, for example, Ten Commandments in first grade, Lord's Prayer in second, and so on.

Among adults, this educational goal can be accomplished through programs that focus on the mastery of Bible content. There are several excellent programs that focus on learning Bible stories, or a knowledgeable teacher can simply accompany a group in reading through the entire Bible. The primary educational goal at this level is to learn the biblical and catechetical story of God's immense mercy for the world, as demonstrated in the core narrative.

A second educational goal is *to think through the story*. If confirmands already have a firm grasp of the biblical story, critical reflection ought to be a major emphasis for confirmation instruction. To think through the story entails introduction to the historical process through which Scripture developed, that is, basic introduction to historical interpretation. It means discovering the nature of myth as a conveyor of God's truth as one thinks about certain Bible stories, for example, Jonah and the whale. It means confronting the apparent discrepancy between what one learns about creation in the first chapters of Genesis and what one is learning about the big bang theory and evolution in science classes at school.

The church must demonstrate a willingness to accompany its members, especially the young, as they critically examine the truth of the Christian faith; while at the same time testifying that such critical thought does not so much diminish as enhance the meaning of Christian truth. The church fails in its educational mission insofar as it hesitates and avoids grappling with these issues. By failing to prepare its youth for reflection on such critical questions, the church unwittingly assures that each generation undergoes a period of disillusionment before some—but only a few—find their way back into its fold.

Adult educational forums are the ideal place to assist all members to reflect critically on the meaning of the Christian faith. Since not all will participate in such ventures, sermons can regularly assist in demonstrating the church's willingness to delve into self-critical examination of its beliefs. Likewise in its publications (for example, a monthly newsletter), a congregation can provide impulses for deepening awareness of the complexity of Christian history and thinking through difficult questions. Classes for new members should place significant emphasis on the importance of lifelong Christian education and provide the opportunity for serious intellectual inquiry.

In accomplishing the goal of encouraging people to think through the faith, members should be exposed to great Christian thinkers from the past and present, those who both analyzed the faith with critical acumen and at the same time maintained deep piety and devotion. Justin Martyr, Augustine, Hildegaard of Bingen, Thomas Aquinas, Theresa of Avila, Martin Luther, Søren Kierkegaard, Dorothy Day, Dietrich Bonhoeffer, and Gustavo Gutiérrez are among those whose reflections on the faith deserve to be widely known. More about the vital witness of Christian saints will be developed in the next section.

Finally, the church must engage its members in the perennial task of *living the faith*. As we have seen, participation in the liturgy provides primary impetus toward this goal. Never do we leave behind our sinful and selfish nature, which limits our ability to embody the Christlike life. Yet those who are mature in faith can demonstrate a powerful congruity between what they profess and how they live. Each sanctified life finds its own expression, given the unique gifts of God and the particular station in God's world. The Spirit of God becomes manifest powerfully in lives humbly consecrated to divine service. The central mark of a saintly life is always the admission of one's sinfulness before God and neighbor, accompanied by joyous reception of God's grace and forgiveness granted in Christ Jesus: "I have been crucified with Christ; and it is no longer I who live, but it is Christ who lives in me" (Gal 2:19-20).

Our education in the Christian faith returns us again and again to the Sunday morning liturgy. The liturgical pattern remains for all of one's life the central location where one is educated in what it means to be a child of God and a member of the Christian community. In the regular rhythm of Word and Sacrament, we learn, think, and live the faith.

Saints Who Followed

Our age is hungry for heroes. Every news story seems to shift away from an analysis of issues and causes to the personalities of those involved. Movie stars, athletes, musicians, politicians, military officers, and announcers each have a particular place in the pantheon of American gods. The values that these heroes represent are glamour, wealth, strength, power, sex appeal, and success. Young people are not the only ones drawn to these as role models, although the tendency may be especially noticeable among them. Heroes from the screen serve as mighty icons in shaping our aspirations and, thereby, our self-image and identity.

Over the generations, Christians have engaged in heated controversy over the place afforded to its "heroes," the saints. Here the term *saint* is not used so much in the generic sense in which all the baptized are saints but in the particular sense that some become exemplary for others in demonstrating the significance of the Christian life. Some argue, with good reason, that the only figure deserving our undivided attention is the person of Jesus alone. Jesus Christ is the exclusive object of our devotion. And in terms of our worship, clearly this position is correct.

While it is theologically accurate to argue that Jesus is and remains the central Christian icon, is there not also room for amazement and inspiration from the example of those who in every generation demonstrated what it means to live a Christian life? Can we not be formed in our own Christian discipleship by studying how the light of Christ has shown in other saintly lives? There is a deep and profound longing for such models. If they are not forthcoming from the church, then heroes will be sought elsewhere and emulated according to values that contradict the faith.

The testimony of the saints offers a tremendous resource for Christian education. Whereas discussion of religious doctrine and theological concepts may be perceived as abstract and irrelevant, we can enliven the discussion of Christian truth through biographical study, demonstrating what the teachings of the church meant to real people at particular moments in history. James W. McClendon is certainly right. Theology as incarnated in a personal biography reveals how ideas do indeed make a difference in how one lives. The dilemmas faced by other Christians as they sought to remain faithful disciples in their own context shed light on our struggle to be faithful here and now.

McClendon has demonstrated this case with reference to the biographies of Dag Hammarskjöld, Martin Luther King Jr., Clarence Jordan, and Charles Ives. He pays strict attention to the central images that guided each journey in faith. For example, Hammarskjöld favored the images of servant, Jesus as Brother, and the "unheard of," while King turned to images of the exodus—Egyptian bondage, the Pharaoh's yoke, and the promised land. Certain guiding images shape a particular way of envisioning and imagining the faith in order to meet the particular challenges of Christian discipleship at a decisive moment in history.

This method can bear fruit as the commitment and example of myriad saints feed the imaginations of Christian people. Saints from biblical times testify to God's presence in diverse contexts: Elijah, Ruth, Jeremiah, Esther, Mary Magdalene, and Barnabas. Each points to a story worth reclaiming. The history of the church is replete with the witness of those committed to following Jesus: Gregory of Nyssa, Macrina, Francis of Assisi, Clare, Margery Kempe, Anselm of Canterbury, John Calvin, Rose of Lima, Ann Lee, Jonathan Edwards, Sojourner Truth, Dietrich Bonhoeffer, and Mother Theresa. To view each life story in the context of the times sheds light on our own lives and times. As we consider these witnesses, what does it mean for us to be disciples of Jesus today?

The lives of the saints demonstrate not only that in every generation there have been those who embodied the faith to meet the challenges of their own times but also that in every age it is the same God and the same Christ to whom the church seeks to remain faithful. Above all, we learn that God has remained faithful to us. Wherever sin threatened the lives of the saints, God's forgiveness was even more abundant. We learn that now it is our turn to appeal to the core images for living faithfully in this generation.

Those who employ biography as a means for Christian education discover vitality absent from discussions of disembodied ideas. Biography provides entrance to the central concepts of the faith that remain vital for Christian identity and mission. Media presentations provide valuable assistance in envisioning the lives of the saints. In the process, Christian people fill their minds with alternative images of heroes, who aid them in discerning *how to live their own lives Christianly.* At worship, we reinforce these images by commemorating the lives of those saints recognized in the liturgical calendar.

The educational emphasis on the lives of the "great" saints should not cause us to overlook the testimony of saints closer to home. There is much wisdom to be discovered where congregations establish mentoring programs among members. Baptismal sponsors can learn what it means to be mentors for their godchild. Confirmands can be assigned mentors to nurture them in faith development. The newly married can be paired with experienced couples who will pray for them and encourage them. The grieving receive consolation and understanding from those who themselves have experienced similar grief.

The work of the saints goes on in every Christian congregation. In groups formed for mutual support, there naturally emerges an educational dimension focusing on a Christian response to life's crises. The relationships that form among members in groups teach volumes about the ongoing incarnation of the faith. It is especially through the example of those who walk with us as mentors and friends that we learn how to live the Christian life. Congregations do well to name, organize, and otherwise foster mentor relationships among members and to recognize these as a valuable component of educational ministry.

Crossings

One of the most impenetrable boundaries of life is the one dividing Sunday morning from the rest of the week. Increasingly in the modern world, the connection between Christian faith and daily life has become broken. The nineteenth century, which saw the industrial revolution flourish, was the same century that witnessed the privatization of the Christian faith. Faith came to be understood as good for families, especially for women and children in domestic life, but Christian commitment had no place in the public world. The implications of this view persist and intensify in our time. Note the relative absence of men from Sunday worship and the startling statistic that correlates continued church involvement by young people with the active participation of their fathers.

At least since the Reformation, the church has elevated this watchword: "the church is the priesthood of all believers." By this, Luther meant to sanctify the vocations of all Christians, placing great importance on the role of all honest workers in ordering and sustaining God's world. Today we sometimes speak of "ministry in daily life" as an expression of this Reformation concern. Nevertheless, to an alarming degree the bifurcation between Sunday morning and the rest of the week remains fixed.

Congregations need to address this gap in their educational ministry. Models exist in the "Crossings" ministry (centered in St. Louis) and the *Connections* program (created by Norma Cook Everist and Nelvin Vos), which have proven invaluable in crossing the boundary between what we profess and the occupations into which we pour out our lifeblood. In these programs, members of congregations are asked to conscientiously juxtapose their faith and their vocations. Many do so for the first time. In a process of explicit reflection, new insight is gained not only into the relevance of the faith for daily life but into the meaning of faith as one's very source of identity. Scripture comes alive as testimony to God's involvement, not in ecclesiastical affairs, but in the lives of people engaged in nothing less than their daily business.

Groups formed for mutual sharing about the interface of faith and daily work can be vital for building the connection between Sunday and Monday. Bible texts can be studied to claim their significance for integrating faith with the daily ethical and interpersonal dilemmas facing Christians in the world. Relationships of mutual support that develop at a profound level grow through intentional efforts to connect the workplace with the sanctuary. Additional groups may evolve that continue to meet for prayer and guidance. People who once believed they were too busy for church begin to see their Christian faith as the necessary foundation for functioning with integrity, learning to deal with failure, and discovering transcendent meaning within the daily grind. The liturgy becomes the lens through which all of life becomes transfigured.

Each of the three emphases discussed in this chapter—the arcane discipline of the early church translated today into the basic goals of learning, thinking, and living the Christian story; the importance of saints as models of the faith; and the connection between Sunday worship and daily life—contributes not only to better Christian education but to the renewal of the church in a post-Christian age. The number-one priority for Christian education in our time is making disciples. While the number of options one can program for Christian education is infinite, the priority on disciple-making contributes directly to the fundamental purpose of the congregation, building Christian identity for the sake of Christ's mission in the world.

FOR FURTHER READING

Benson, Peter L., and Carolyn H. Eklin. *Effective Christian Education: A National Study of Protestant Congregations. A Summary Report of Faith, Loyalty, and Congregational Life.* Minneapolis: Search Institute, 1990.

Carter, Craig A. *Rethinking Christ and Culture: A Post-Christendom Perspective.* Grand Rapids: Brazos, 2007.

Diehl, William E. *Ministry in Daily Life: A Practical Guide for Congregations.* Annapolis Junction: Alban Institute, 1996.

Everist, Norma Cook, ed. *Christian Education as Evangelism.* Minneapolis: Fortress Press, 2007.

Everist, Norma Cook. *The Church as Learning Community: A Comprehensive Guide to Christian Education.* Nashville: Abingdon, 2002.

Everist, Norma Cook, and Nelvin Vos. *Connections: Faith and Life.* Chicago: Evangelical Lutheran Church in America, Division for Congregational Ministries, 1997.

Foss, Michael W. *The Disciple's Joy: Six Practices for Spiritual Growth.* Minneapolis: Augsburg Fortress, 2007.

Fowler, James W. *Stages of Faith and Religious Development: Implications for Church, Education and Society.* New York: Crossroad, 1991.

Groome, Thomas H. *Educating for Life: A Spiritual Vision for Every Teacher and Parent.* New York: Crossroad, 2001.

McClendon, James William, Jr. *Biography as Theology: How Life Stories Can Remake Today's Theology.* Nashville: Abingdon, 1974.

Mead, Loren B. *The Once and Future Church: Reinventing the Congregation for a New Mission Frontier.* Bethesda, Md.: Alban Institute, 1991.

Rite of Christian Initiation of Adults: Study Edition. Prepared by International Commission on English in Liturgy and Bishops' Committee on the Liturgy. Washington, D.C.: United States Catholic Conference, 1988.

FOR REFLECTION AND DISCUSSION

1. What does "disciple-making" mean to you? What are some of the central ways your congregation makes disciples?

2. What signs do you see that we are living in a post-Christian era? What changes does the church need to make in such a time?

3. In what ways does your congregation help people learn the Christian story? Think the Christian story? Live the Christian story?

4. Which saints of God have had the most influence on your life as a Christian? Why? Which saints of God should be more well-known in your congregation?

5. How does your congregation help people make the connection between what happens at church on Sunday and their daily lives? How could you improve at this?

Chapter Seven

Life in Community: Friends of the Crucified

On Maundy Thursday, the liturgy engages the congregation in two profound ritual actions. The first takes place only on this night. Girded with a towel, a minister takes water and bends down to wash feet. This ritual reenacts the night before Jesus' crucifixion, when he humbled himself to wash the feet of his disciples.

Prior to the foot-washing ritual, a passage of Scripture is read from the Gospel of John chapter 13: "I give you a new commandment, that you love one another. Just as I have loved you, you also should love one another. By this everyone will know that you are my disciples, if you have love for one another" (vv. 34-35). Elaborating on this theme in 15:12-15, Jesus declares: "This is my commandment, that you love one another as I have loved you. No one has greater love than this, to lay down one's life for one's friends. You are my friends if you do what I command you. I do not call you servants any longer, because the servant does not know what the master is doing; but I have called you friends, because I have made known to you everything that I have heard from my Father."

The second ritual action of Maundy Thursday is the gathering around the table for Holy Communion. Bread and wine are shared; this is the very body and blood of Christ, in remembrance of all Jesus suffered to demonstrate the depths of God's love for us.

Together, these dramatic rituals, the washing of feet accompanied by a reading about love and the gathering together around the table, establish the norm for the communal life in a congregation. Friendship with the crucified Jesus serves as the basis for our friendship with one another. When we view one another properly, we see the other in the light of what Jesus suffered for each of us on the cross. We understand one another as common recipients of divine grace as we partake together at the Lord's Table. Even more, we comprehend that our only mission is exemplified in the washing of feet, the weary feet of those within the congregation and the feet of many others whom we invite to be refreshed in Christian fellowship.

The Meaning of Christian Friendship

To describe members of a congregation as "friends" can lead to serious misunderstanding. Friendship in Christ is not founded on feelings of closeness to one another. Nor is it based on one's attraction to certain kindred personalities. In the surrounding culture, friendship is based almost exclusively upon what one finds appealing in another person. Friendship often is based on what friends can offer to each other to achieve self-fulfillment. Friendship may be reduced to seeking out those who can help satisfy my personal needs.

In the church, by contrast, we must learn to think christologically about friendship. Friendship begins with Jesus graciously naming us as his friends. Those who seek to follow Jesus and keep his commandments are given the privilege of understanding themselves as Jesus' friends. This sounds at first rather cozy. Me and Jesus: friends. That is all too cozy, until we notice those others whom Jesus also calls friends. To be summoned into friendship with Jesus is to discover ourselves in the company of all those who live as Jesus' disciples. Many of these are people with whom we would never associate by natural inclination.

As Dietrich Bonhoeffer wrote in *Life Together*, Christian community is not a dream of our own making. Christian friendship does not come into existence according to my own ideal expectations but rather at God's beckoning. One of the greatest threats to genuine Christian community is the "visionary dreaming" by which I establish my own standards for the community rather than allowing the spirit of Christ to create the community according to God's own specifications.

One of the deepest mysteries of Christian friendship occurs as Jesus Christ himself meets us in the form of the other. Article 4 of the Smalcald Articles names five means of grace by which the gospel of Jesus Christ is mediated to us, one of these being "the mutual conversation and consolation of brothers and sisters." Jesus promised in Matthew 18:20: "Where two or three are gathered in my name, I am there among them." As Christians speak to one another in mutual faith, sharing mutual concerns and addressing one another under the gospel's promise of forgiveness, Jesus is really present among them. Thereby we discover the miracle that we are "little Christs" for one another (Luther).

M. Scott Peck retells a powerful tale, "The Rabbi's Gift," at the beginning of his book, *The Different Drum: Community Making and Peace.* A once thriving monastery has over the decades been reduced to five aged monks. The abbot broods over the decimation of the once vital order, pondering its imminent demise. Going to the woods to pray, the abbot consults with an old rabbi there on retreat. As they commiserate about days gone by, the abbot beseeches the rabbi for advice. The rabbi's only cryptic word is this: "One of you is the Messiah."

Returning to the monastery, the abbot shares this word with the brothers. In consternation, none of them can believe this could be true: they know one another's faults all too well! Yet slowly and surely there develops a profound sense of respect for one another, just in the slight chance the rabbi could be right. What if one of the other brothers indeed could be the Messiah? The new sense of respect and self-dignity begins to attract new visitors to the dying monastery. One by one, new postulants enter, restoring the order as a center of hope in the lives of many. What wonders are wrought by the conviction that in my neighbor I meet Jesus Christ!

The mystery of friendship in Christ goes yet deeper. As we live together in Christian community, Jesus promises to be present, mediating our relationships. Yet we are not the ones with the power to decide when and where Jesus becomes manifest. Rather, as Jesus indicated in the parable of the great judgment in Matthew 25:31-46, it is at the moment we would least expect it, among those who are the "least of these," in the person of the hungry, sick, or imprisoned, that Jesus comes to encounter us. This passage summons us to extend Christian friendship to those at the very margins of "decent" society. To establish a congregation as an association of the "like-minded" runs the imminent danger of excluding Christ as the one who meets us in the form of the unlovely. We are summoned to be a church that is radically egalitarian in its composition, inviting exactly those scorned by the world.

Finally, Christian friendship entails communion with the crucified. A theology of the cross insists that Jesus is never more present than in those very places where he appears to be most absent. Crucified as a criminal on Golgotha, Jesus was rejected by all decent society and even abandoned by his disciples. Yet exactly here God was manifest in our world, taking up the cause of the world's abandoned and rejected ones. Christian friendship takes up the cause of Jesus by ministering to those in acute pain and suffering. Friendship in the church of Jesus Christ searches for those places of service where no one else dares go—among those most excluded from human company. Here it is that one can be assured that Jesus Christ is already present, waiting for a cruciform church to appear.

Egalitarian Communion

Members of a congregation do not have to like one another, although that is always nice. They do, however, have the command from Jesus to love one another. As in a family with several children, they don't have to like one another. But God has thrust them together into this configuration, and they are compelled to learn the true nature of love, not as a romantic ideal but a daily challenge. In a family, there is no question about choosing to belong or not belong. Belonging is a given, and one must simply learn to get along with each other's quirks and bad manners. The church, like a family, serves as a clinic for discovering what it means to be brothers and sisters.

The primary arena where we learn the art of Christian community is the liturgy. By our common participation in the rituals of confession, absolution, prayer, passing the peace, and sharing Eucharist—as we imagine and enact together the kingdom—we see one another differently, that is, as we truly are in God's eyes. The distinctions that divide and separate us according to the standards of the world are radically altered by our common baptism in the name of Jesus. Neither age, nor gender, nor race, nor sexual orientation, nor wealth, nor job status is of any consequence (Gal 3:28). The only relevant information is that we are all people for whom Christ died.

When the leadership of worship is shared with others through the active involvement of many assisting ministers as ushers, greeters, acolytes, cantors, choir members, lectors, musicians, intercessors, and Communion assistants, another key aspect of Christian fellowship is revealed. The people of God are a gifted people; spiritual gifts abound in the life of the community. God has granted each one special gifts symbolized by the service rendered by the various members at worship. The standard by which these gifts are measured is the contribution made to the common good. The gifts God lends are not for personal aggrandizement but for the mutual up building of the body of Christ. Paul's dictum regarding spiritual gifts continues to instruct us: "The greatest of these is love" (1 Cor 13:13).

While the spiritual gifts of the community are symbolized by mutuality in the leadership of liturgy, the sharing of gifts is extended by the mutual care of members throughout the week. Relationships of friendship are witnessed in the concern shown for those members of the body of Christ in special need: the sick, the dying, the grieving, the divorcing, the unemployed, the hungry, the single parents, the infertile couples, the spiritually confused, the troubled youth, and so forth. The people for whom we pray in the intercessory prayers become the recipients of spiritual care.

As members of a congregation live together and experience various needs, they discover the particular gifts of the various individuals. One is gifted in sewing, another in carpentry, yet another in leading small groups. Each individual has unique charisms to offer. An assets approach to congregational ministry, based on appreciative inquiry, allows the church to recognize and affirm the peculiar gifts of each one. Unlike society, which marginalizes all those who are not "normal" (that is, young, successful, and healthy), the congregation's life in community values and practices an egalitarian communion, in which the gifts of each are employed for common benefit. The community that gathers around Jesus is a motley crew, unlovely in the world's eyes but saints according to divine promise.

This is not to say there are no conflicts among members of the Christian community. Tensions do arise both from chafing personalities and from differing opinions about decisions to be made. It is always tragic when congregation members cannot resolve the differences that divide them. Slapping labels on those with whom one is in conflict is never helpful. Instead, the choice for mediation that assists us in viewing issues from the perspective of the other, while perhaps not always resolving the difference, can teach us to respect one another and preserve the overall aim of promoting the common good. Where antagonism leads to the division of the congregation, all parties need to confess their own sins and beg for God's gracious forgiveness. In situations of chronic conflict, the expertise of trained interim pastors may be crucial to the healing process.

Prayer serves to powerfully create and sustain Christian friendship within the congregation. While intercessory prayer remains integral to Sunday worship, mutual prayer for one another continues throughout the week. The constant offering of intercessions for one another reflects the divine context in which the congregation lives (Phil 1:3-5). The special needs of the sick, grieving, and distressed are brought to God in prayer, and we ourselves are shaped in the process. Prayer moves us to acts of charity on behalf of those for whom we pray. We visit, call, or send a meal. Anger is diffused in prayer; those who are praying for one another cannot easily harbor resentment.

Prayer for the congregation leads to transformed action on one another's behalf. Through shared participation in worship and mutual concern rooted in prayer, a congregation becomes, in the parlance of the Quakers, a society of friends. One definition of a friend is someone with whom you enjoy "wasting" time. Where caring relationships develop among members, there is heaven on earth. So too there can be extreme disillusionment where the church fails to live up to its potential as a loving community. Many have become alienated from the church due to its failure to care. Indeed, for its failure to embody genuine community, the church must continually confess its sins and plead for God's mercy. One acute danger of Christian friendship is that the community ceases to welcome the outsider. Members become so familiar with one another that they fail to extend fellowship beyond a closed circle. The standard of egalitarian communion fails to be normative even in the sanctuary.

Christian community begins and ends with the friendship of God in Christ with us. For Jesus' sake, we call one another friends. This means patterning the relationships of the church after the manner of Jesus: egalitarian, compassionate, listening, serving, forgiving, celebrating each member's gifts, cruciform, caring for the least. Friendship always remains both an incomparable joy for which to give thanks and a responsibility for bearing another's burdens. As it is in our own friendship with Jesus, so may it be in the communion of saints!

Pastor and People

One way of understanding the pastoral office is to view the pastor as public representative of the friendship of God among the people. The pastor is called to proclaim publicly God's gospel friendship in Word and Sacrament. Furthermore, the pastor is called to embody the friendship of God in relationships with members of a congregation, especially through pastoral care.

The pastor, by virtue of her/his office, holds one of the most privileged positions in all of society. Invited into the lives of people at moments of great vulnerability and joy, the pastor serves as a representative of God in everything that is said and done. While one should resist losing one's personal identity to the requirements of an office, graciously living out the role that inevitably comes with the office opens great opportunities for ministry. The work of a pastor is a vocation, not a job that can be set aside at the end of the work day. Whether at the local fast food restaurant or shopping at a mall, members and nonmembers alike will see the person as pastor, God's representative.

This not only places a burden of responsibility on the shoulders of the person called to ordained ministry, but insofar as a family is involved, it can also encumber the entire family system. Spouses and children of pastors suffer from a stigma that must first be acknowledged before it can be creatively addressed. While it is important to maintain one's integrity and not surrender to unrealistic demands, the pastor's family must learn to adjust to its public identity as graciously as possible. Support from other clergy families, understanding from sensitive congregation members, and a sense of humor are assets in this process. The pastor's family must be very intentional about negotiating the boundary situation in which they find themselves. Seeking pastoral care from outside their own congregation can be a constructive resource.

The privilege afforded the pastor, being invited to enter into the private hurts and celebrations of God's people, entails great responsibility. As a giver of pastoral care, the pastor must be trained in listening and responding to human need. The pastor, like the suffering servant of Isaiah, is acquainted with sorrows and familiar with grief (53:3). Unlike the friends of Job, the pastor refrains from answering in platitudes, and instead allows the full measure of human emotion to find expression. Sometimes this means the anger people feel toward God will be projected at one's own person as God's representative. In these cases, one must remain clear that this is a function of the office one bears rather than a personal attack.

In seeking to offer appropriate pastoral care, the pastor should not presume to be the master of all human dilemmas. Through experience, the pastor will be exposed to a wide range of human problems and predicaments. To properly distinguish between law and gospel has implications for pastoral care. A word of judgment may sometimes be necessary to attempt to redirect a person from a destructive path. Most often, the pastor will seek ways to make the comfort and forgiveness of God known in the lives of distressed people. One of life's greatest needs is hope for a better future, and the pastor can provide such, for in the friendship of God there is always hope. Should the situation call for skills beyond the competence of the pastor, one mark of wisdom is to admit one's limits and know the available resources in order to make a helpful referral.

With the pastor's privileged access to people's lives comes also the requirement not to use one's authority destructively. This can occur in conversations with members who do not share the same level of knowledge as the educated pastor. It can occur in meetings where group dynamics single out certain individuals for ostracism if they oppose the pastor. Most tragically, it can occur in relationships with parishioners who become objects of sexual manipulation. Sexual contact with a congregation member *always* constitutes a violation of pastoral trust and is destructive to life in community. The sacred trust necessary for the pastor to serve as representative of God's friendship is betrayed. Abuse of pastoral power is always a cause for church discipline. The healing process within a congregation after a violation of pastoral sexual ethics is always lengthy and arduous.

One of the endangered practices in modern society is that of making house calls. In part, this practice has been endangered exactly by the concern for observing clear sexual boundaries. In meeting with individuals, visitation now means establishing clear structures, including accountability to the larger community by monitoring where and when visits take place. This means fewer home visits and more meetings with members at the church during regular office hours, when the setting can be monitored by others present at the church. The reality of this ethical practice places new restraints on visiting people in their homes.

At the same time, home visitation by the pastor serves as symbol of the friendship of God in the many cases where this is not a violation of proper boundaries. While scheduling around the activities of busy members itself may present a challenge, the value of such visitation is finally worth the hassle. A foundation of trust to undergird ministry is established as a pastor is welcomed as guest, and friendship is extended. The focus of pastoral calling is not only to learn the life stories of the members of the congregation but to communicate the friendship of God with each person and family, especially in response to stories of pain. This entails conversation about the spiritual needs of those visited as well as about physical health. Taking time for Bible reading, hymn singing, and prayer as part of a pastoral visit communicates the nearness and mercy of God for those in each home.

Pastoral friendship also means faithful and prompt response in times of acute need. Those hospitalized, anticipating surgery, grieving loss, or in any type of crisis need the reassurance of God's presence by contact from their pastor and other Christians. Though such occasions always come as interruptions to the planned schedule, they are the very times when God becomes mysteriously present in a remarkable manner. This is the promise of the cross of Jesus Christ. The pastor is privileged to witness to the unfailing power of the crucified God to sustain us in life's most challenging hour. Sharing prayer or Holy Communion places the entire crisis in a different perspective, that of God's boundless kindness and friendship. Pastors who respond faithfully to the acute needs of people offer authentic testimony to the goodness and mercy of the One they represent.

Telephone and email messages provide other important avenues for extending the friendship of God among the members of a congregation, especially in the age of the cell phone. A quick phone call, text message, or email in the course of the day does much to buoy another's spirit. People appreciate being remembered, whether it is on a birthday, anniversary, retirement, or some other notable occasion. Those recently hospitalized can give a follow-up report over the phone or by email. Contact with new or lapsed members can be initiated. Creative use of the phone and email can serve to broaden pastoral ministry in communicating God's friendship among a people.

The purpose of congregational ministry among youth is not to create a ghetto of younger aged persons but to integrate them into the larger community life and ministry of the congregation. Too often, youth ministry degenerates into "activities" to keep the "young people" occupied and off the streets. The youth group functions more like a social club than a vital dimension of the entire congregation's life. The youth of a congregation are not "its future" as many are wont to say, but already baptized and full members of the body of Christ.

In subtle and sometimes overt ways, most congregations communicate a second-class status through their youth programs. They hire an "assistant" pastor to entertain the youth. Or they coerce members to take over as youth sponsors. They hold a "Youth Sunday" or have special services for the youth. While in and of themselves none of these practices are inherently bad, they communicate a mindset that robs the church of the plenitude of gifts that youth bring to make the body of Christ whole and healthy. The gifts that uniquely talented young people bring to the church are needed by the entire congregation and should not be relegated to a youth enclave.

From a young age, children should be welcome in the congregational community. Children need to grow up knowing their congregation as a place where they belong as cherished persons who share the identity of baptized children of God with all the other members. Children, as part of the congregation, should be welcome at worship, even if this means they sometimes "interrupt" the proceedings. There is no reason families with children should be expected to occupy the back pews of the sanctuary when the action is taking place up front. Encourage them to sit toward the front! Hymns that children enjoy can be sung by the entire congregation. Children's sermons can be based on the regular lectionary and make points applicable to members of every age rather than merely offering cute (and usually trite) entertainment. Children can serve as acolytes, choir members, greeters, ushers, and readers, having received appropriate training and attained the level of competence expected of all members.

Children can be welcomed at Holy Communion, if not by receiving the elements, then by means of a personal blessing. Preparation for the Lord's Table can be introduced at an earlier age than many congregations now practice. As soon as they can read, children can be presented their own Bibles within the context of the worship service. Younger children display an enthusiasm for Bible reading that often puts their elders to shame. Children should be frequently reminded of the importance of their own baptism as they participate in the order of baptism for others, especially babies. As they practice the liturgy on a regular basis, children soon become active participants in the eucharistic drama. There is deep joy for those who lead worship to look into the congregation and see children singing along with the rest!

By the time one reaches the age of confirmation instruction, children should already be at home in the congregation's life. As young people are challenged to think more deeply about the Christian faith during confirmation classes, the curriculum does well to leave space for confirmands to bring experiences from daily life to the classroom. These can be addressed from the standpoint of how one might respond to a particular issue as a Christian. As the friendship of God is experienced in the relationship of confirmands with their teachers and pastor, the community established among them will encourage ongoing participation even when the formal classes are completed.

Postconfirmation youth need to be fully incorporated into the congregation's ministry. While the youth may continue to hold separate meetings, it is essential that they also be intentionally and fully included in congregational worship, education, community life, and programs. Young people are often extremely willing and enthusiastic participants in service projects to meet the needs of others. Young people can be encouraged to participate actively in congregational committees and celebrations. A fine symbol of equal status is to elect young members to serve on the governing council.

Youth ministry in the congregation should not be separate from the rest of ministry but a vital dimension of the whole. Where youth are visibly present in every aspect of congregational life, there the friendship of God is seen in a more egalitarian communion. Children and youth are friends of God who need to become friends with members of every age. Mutual friendship between young people and their elders offers tangible evidence of God's kingdom in the company of the One who himself did not cast off but welcomed children (Mark 9:37).

Pastors, by virtue of their unique role as God's representatives, have the opportunity to welcome others into the community of God. Whether on Sunday morning (before, during, or after worship) or at other times during the week (as one speaks to people in the office, over the phone, or on visits), the pastor's hospitality is a matter of great importance. Not only does it matter in terms of how people evaluate a particular individual as pastor, but even more importantly, it makes a significant difference in how people perceive God. This is both a tremendous responsibility and also an extraordinary opportunity. A pastor is invited into the crises of human life in a unique way. Being a pastor is both the best and worst of vocations for this very reason. For those so called, the joy far surpasses the burden!

In order to maintain one's perspective in ministry, the pastor needs spiritual support to be sustained in God's friendship: caring relationships with other clergy, congregational support committees, regular participation in continuing education, a circle of support extending beyond the congregation, good exercise habits, and a healthy prayer life. To lose one's own experience of the divine friendship is to lose the very soul of one's ministry. Should one reach a crisis in one's sense of calling, a pastor needs to be humble in reaching out for professional counseling, the very thing one would recommend to parishioners in need. What may first appear as a devastating personal crisis can be transformed by the power of God into an occasion for entering even more deeply into the pain of others. Renewed by a vivid awareness of God's living presence through prayer, study, and collegial relationships, a pastor is able to serve as representative of God's friendship in the midst of a grateful people.

FOR FURTHER READING

Bonhoeffer, Dietrich. *Life Together and Prayerbook of the Bible.* Translated by Daniel W. Bloesch and James H. Burtness. Dietrich Bonhoeffer Works 5 Minneapolis: Fortress Press, 1996.

Bruesehoff, Richard J., and Phyllis Wiederhoeft. *Pastor and People: Making Mutual Ministry Work.* Minneapolis: Augsburg Fortress, 2003.

Fortune, Marie M. *Is Nothing Sacred? The Story of a Pastor, the Women He Sexually Abused, and the Congregation He Nearly Destroyed.* Eugene, Ore.: Wipf & Stock, 2008.

Friedman, Edward. *Generation to Generation: Family Process in Church and Synagogue.* New York: Guilford, 1985.

Haight, Roger. *Christian Community in History: Ecclesial Existence.* New York: Continuum, 2008.

Hinson, E. Glenn. *Spiritual Preparation for Christian Leadership.* Nashville: The Upper Room, 1999.

Nouwen, Henri J. M. *In the Name of Jesus: Reflections on Christian Leadership.* New York: Crossroad, 1992.

Olson, Mark A. *Moving Beyond Church Growth: An Alternative Vision for Congregations*. Minneapolis: Augsburg Fortress, 2001.

Palmer, Parker J. *The Promise of Paradox: A Celebration of Contradictions in Christian Life*. San Francisco: Jossey-Bass, 2008.

Peck, M. Scott. *The Different Drum: Community Making and Peace*. New York: Touchstone, 1998.

Wadell, Paul J. *Becoming Friends: Worship, Justice, and the Practice of Christian Friendship*. Grand Rapids: Brazos, 2002.

Whitehead, James D. *Community of Faith: Crafting Christian Communities Today*. Lincoln: AuthorHouse, 2001.

FOR REFLECTION AND DISCUSSION

1. What is the significance of the washing of feet during worship or at other times in the life of the church? What implications does this practice have for the life of your congregation?

2. What is distinctive about "Christian" friendship that makes it different from other forms of friendship? How well does your congregation practice the friendship of the Crucified in its community life?

3. How egalitarian and diverse is your congregation and why is that so? How can you imagine expanding the diversity as a sign of the kingdom of God?

4. What are the primary involvements of children and youth in your congregation? How can these younger members of the body of Christ be more fully incorporated into the life of the community?

5. How does the relationship between pastor and people in your congregation embody the mutual care between Jesus Christ and the church? Give thanks for the positive examples that you name.

Chapter Eight

Stewardship:
God Owns Everything

Churches and Sunday schools in generations past were accustomed to sing as the offering was collected: "We give thee but Thine own, whate'er the gift may be; all that we have is Thine alone, a trust, O Lord from thee." Today, many congregations pray a prayer like this, following the offering of gifts: "Blessed are you, O God, maker of all things. Through your goodness you have blessed us with these gifts: our selves, our time, and our possessions. Use us, and what we have gathered, in feeding the world with your love, through the one who gave himself for us, Jesus Christ, our Savior and Lord." In both cases something radical has been uttered: The things that I claim to possess are not my own! Indeed, the very life within me does not belong to me. All that I am and have are, when truly seen, gifts from God—God's possession, not my own.

In our times, the starting point for all Christian stewardship is the question of ownership. In the liturgy, we claim that God is the one who endows us with every gift, every possession, even the breath of life. Yet such an assertion runs against the grain of everything an acquisitive culture teaches us about the meaning and purpose of life. In this chapter, we examine the question of ownership as the key issue in developing the theme of stewardship. Tithing is advocated as a means by which to begin to check one's idolatry. Last, the theme of "caring" is articulated as a comprehensive rubric for interpreting the responsibility of the Christian life.

Understanding oneself as steward grounds self-identity firmly in trusting God above all things. "Being in Christ," as formed through worship, shaped by Christian education, and nurtured in Christian community, becomes the orientation by which one views the entirety of one's life. Those who see themselves as "stewards of God's mysteries" (1 Cor 4:1) find themselves out of step with the prevailing order, structured on the accumulation of material possessions above all things. Instead of taking credit for one's own earnings, one lives in gratitude for God's bountiful goodness. Furthermore, one assumes responsibility that the world's goods be shared for the benefit of all, beginning with those most acutely in need.

Ownership

Legally speaking, we own many things. Our system of law has detailed provisions for defining and defending the rights of private property. When purchasing a house, for example, the letter of the law must be followed in order to guarantee that the transaction is properly conducted and recorded in a way that will satisfy a court of law. Similarly, the title for an automobile is carefully monitored by the state. Even for minor purchases, one is wise to retain the sales slip to prove payment.

The system by which we earn wages, make purchases, save or invest money, and accumulate capital is pervasive. There exists a sense of general well-being when the stock market increases—and a shocking downturn in well-being when the stock market fails. Economic growth (GNP) has become the primary measure by which we judge the success of a presidential administration. Self-worth is evaluated on the basis of net worth. A stigma is attached to the unemployed and welfare recipients, those who do not or cannot produce. Advertising looms on every possible horizon, beckoning us to see our primary identity according to what we consume.

Theologically speaking, however, we own nothing. "The earth is the Lord's and all that is in it, the world, and those who live in it" (Ps 24:1). What we dare to confess liturgically is that *God is the owner of the entire world;*

this includes my life, time, energy, and property. This is true about every person on earth. To God as creator and sustainer of all things we owe our gratitude and thanksgiving for what we have, provisions from God's own hand.

In the ministry of Jesus and the earliest church, we see evidence of this theological understanding of ownership. Jesus tells his disciples to travel lightly, taking nothing for the journey except a staff (symbol of itinerancy); no bread, no bag, no money in their belts, not even a change of clothes. The disciples were to depend upon the hospitality of others for their maintenance, returning the good news of the kingdom (Mark 6:7-13). Similarly, the church of Jerusalem is remembered in Acts for the practice of sharing: "No one claimed private ownership of any possessions, but everything they owned was held in common" (4:32). This is not to say that there were no Christians who held substantial wealth. But it does raise the question on whose behalf one administers one's possessions.

The essential meaning of *stewardship* is that the steward holds and administers property on behalf of another. The steward is held responsible for neither squandering nor mismanaging what belongs to another. In every case, however, it is clear that the steward is not the owner but the responsible agent taking care of a possession precious to the superior. This symbol, taken from economic practices of the ancient world, speaks powerfully regarding our proper attitude to property as well. Theologically speaking, God is the owner and we are stewards, answerable to the owner for our management of what does not belong to us.

The contrast between this theological understanding of possessions and the prevalent legal approach that dominates our culture creates a profound dissonance for those who belong to Christ. It means that Christians live in an acute tension with the values of the culture in which they are embedded. The constant temptation is to rationalize according to the conventional norms of earning, acquiring, consuming, and owning. To abandon such measures of worth is to commit an act of heresy against the ruling orthodoxy of economics and the good life. There exists no easy resolution of this dilemma. Still today, one cannot serve God and mammon at the same time (Luke 16:13).

To assume the role of a steward with relationship to the things of the world is to reorient the entirety of one's outlook. The ultimate source of my security is not located in earning capacity, savings accounts, investments, or insurance policies. Like the birds of the air and the lilies of the field, the final source of my security rests in the hands of a benevolently providing God (Matt 6:25-33). Anxiety over food and clothing is wasted. Rather, keeping one's eye on the kingdom supplants all other concerns. Such an attitude is perceived as infinitely impractical and even subversive of the status quo. This may be true. It can also sound like an excuse for sloth. Yet this it is not.

The steward, viewing the things of the earth not as the owner, turns eyes away from preoccupation with the self and is free to see the pressing needs of the neighbor. What replaces my self-concern is genuine concern for the other. No longer is it permissible to cling to the ephemeral belief that each individual's selfish striving will miraculously work out for the benefit of all (Adam Smith). Rather, the priority of the steward becomes the readiness to respond to those most in need, the least of the brothers and sisters (Matt 25:31-46). In our age of ecological devastation, this includes responsiveness to the needs of the earth itself. Indeed, the responsibility of the steward is to advocate a preferential option for the poor—the homeless, the hungry, the powerless, and the very ecosphere that sustains us all. The steward undertakes such advocacy not for the sake of some political agenda but as an integral aspect of kingdom responsibility, the kingdom belonging to God.

The energy once directed toward self-enhancement and self-promotion does not dissipate. By the power of the Spirit and in the company of the Christian community, that energy is instead redirected. Within the established system, this means that I continue to work diligently but now as one accountable to the authority of God. My self-worth is not based on the amount I am able to accumulate—that is, the one with the most toys does not "win"—but derives from my faith in the gracious love of the God who created me and all that exists. The profit from my labors becomes the capital that I administer as a steward on behalf of the one who provided it. The overriding concern in managing the portion of God's bounty assigned to me is how I employ this wealth on behalf of others, especially those most in need. What better motivation for diligent and responsible employment could one imagine! Yet the entire enterprise shifts from an egocentric to a theocentric perspective.

Stewardship can never become an all-encompassing approach to life until we liberate it from the ghetto of annual campaigns to balance congregational budgets. Such campaigns may well be a necessary administrative function of congregational life, especially given our present method of operation. But stewardship means far more, that is, the surrender of all that I have to God and God alone.

Tithing: A Check on Idolatry

Those who take seriously the call to view their livelihood and goods as God's possession may find themselves in a dilemma. First, there is the issue of guilt. How does one appease one's guilt for the plenty that is enjoyed when the world is marked by such radical disparity between "haves" and "have nots"? The law of fairness and equity requires dis-ease as one perceives how many billions of human beings suffer daily in want.

Yet the gospel will not allow us to remain paralyzed by guilt, whether it be prompted by what we have done or what we have left undone. Instead, the gospel of Jesus Christ sets us free from being frozen by the magnitude of the world's problems to function within the realm of responsibility afforded to us. God's steward manages the assigned property with skill and responsibility regardless of how others manage the lot assigned to them. Faithfulness to the charge of the owner is the steward's chief aim, not success in eradicating enormous and apparently intractable problems on a global scale. A steward assumes responsibility in the freedom of one who knows the grace and forgiveness of God in Jesus Christ.

A second aspect of the dilemma facing the steward is the discrepancy between the economic values of the world and those of the kingdom. The tension is dramatic between a life lived by the standard of accumulation and the kingdom's norm of sharing. In order to survive as a steward, one will need to return often to the sanctuary, asking who it is we worship. At worship, one's identity as a citizen of the kingdom is renewed. Within the community of the church, one discovers encouragement for swimming against the culture's stream of acquisitiveness and consumption.

A third question is where to begin. Especially with regard to personal finances, this can be a delicate matter. There is one obvious reason why it is so terribly difficult to speak about money in the church: when we talk about money, we touch upon that which is *God's real rival for our allegiance*. In this society it is money that serves as our greatest idol. While we mock ancient peoples for their ignorance in "worshiping" statues, we fail to acknowledge the idolatry inherent in our attitude toward the almighty dollar. As the writing on the bill announces, "In God we trust." In this culture, life revolves around maximization of economic advantage. Generations from now, archaeologists will discern that the greatest monuments of this age were not cathedrals but shopping malls and corporate skyscrapers. What does this testify about us?

Ginger Anderson-Larson has made a convincing case that our attitudes toward money are the result of a long and effective formation process taught to us by our culture. She argues for the value of taking a personal inventory of one's own relationship to money through the preparation of a "money autobiography." Such a process challenges us to ask core theological questions: What is God's desire for me in relationship to money? When Jesus teaches that where one's treasure is, there will one's heart be also, where is your treasure and where is your heart? (Matt 6:19-22).

If we are to become grateful stewards of what God has given us, the veil of silence surrounding money needs to be disrobed. Through a series of insightful questions, a money autobiography helps us examine our own convictions regarding money and to discover where these values came from. We are challenged to reflect upon the legacy we have inherited from others regarding our relationship to money: Is this the legacy we hope to pass down to the next generation? We are invited to pray about money and our relationship to money, bringing our struggles with the idolatry of money to God.

Anderson-Larson writes: "Sharing, in verbal form, your money autobiography with a trusted confidant, friend, spiritual director, or pastor will increase its potential to bear fruit in your life. To entrust your story to another creates a form of 'holy ground' in which the Holy Spirit's presence can not only be felt, but experienced as empowering in the ongoing work of discerning what this means for daily life and daily work."

The place to begin, if one is serious about the stewardship of money, is with the tithe. While tithing is an ancient practice whose roots can be traced to the law codes of Israel, it is not the purpose here to justify tithing with proof texts. If anything, Jesus' criticism of the Pharisees for their perfunctory tithing ought to make us wary of the practice (Matt 23:23). Instead, there are important theological reasons to support tithing as a reasonable and realizable first step in checking our impulse toward the idolatry of money.

Tithing ought never to be imposed as a requirement. The dangers of a legalistic approach are real. God's love is free and merciful. God makes the sun to shine and rain to fall on all without discrimination. Tithing will not assist one to receive a special blessing from God. Tithing does not make one a better Christian than someone else who does not.

The reason for considering the tithe is for the sake of organizing an assault on one's idolatry of money. If God is indeed the owner of all that has been apportioned to me, then my only proper response is thanksgiving and gratitude for all God has provided. This certainly includes my time and talents. But it also means my finances. To God belongs not just 10 percent but the entire 100 percent of what I have. In order to begin to loosen the vise grip that money has on our lives, however, one may choose to commit to the tithe as a spiritual practice. It is as if one says, "I intend to direct my loyalty and pledge my allegiance to God above all things. As a token of this commitment, I offer a tithe of my income to the work of the kingdom."

Some might choose to gradually adjust to this level of giving. Others might decide to take an abrupt plunge. Still others might in time move well beyond ten percent to larger amounts. There is a degree to which the ability to give is a spiritual gift that differs among us. The final purpose of tithing is not how much one gives but the attitude of gratefulness to God. The aim is to establish worship of God as the highest priority. Tithing is a spiritual discipline for setting one's financial house in order, rendering to God the things that are God's, that is, everything one is and has (Mark 12:17).

One consequence of the widespread practice of tithing in the church would be to make available enormous sums of money for the sake of mission. This money could enhance not only the work of local congregations but global mission, starting new congregations domestically, hunger programs, theological education, and a variety of other forms of service to humanity. The giving of the tithe need not be directed only to the church but could be offered for other charitable causes as well.

While advocating tithing may stir up objections of many kinds, the fundamental issue in our time is idolatry. Joshua once issued the challenge to the people of Israel: "Choose this day whom you will serve, whether the gods your ancestors served in the region beyond the River or the gods of the Amorites in whose land you are living" (Josh 24:15). Tithing is a central Christian practice through which we might again answer with Joshua: "As for me and my household, we will serve the Lord."

Caring

"We care because God first cared for us" (cf. 1 John 4:19). Translating the Greek word *agápē* as "care" instead of "love" discloses dimensions of meaning easily lost in a culture where talk of "love" is cheap. God's love for us does not come cheaply. Its fullest expression comes in the person of Jesus, whose relationships to others were marked by care and whose death on the cross revealed the ultimate act of caring: to lay down one's life for another. As we discuss stewardship as a matter of caring, we do so in acknowledgment that God is the paradigmatic caregiver, who cares for us in order that we might care for others.

In a beautiful and classic book, *On Caring*, Milton Mayeroff describes the purpose of caring as providing for the growth and development of another person. Caring is not performed as an act of manipulation. It does not occur for the satisfaction of one's own unmet needs. Rather, caring unfolds for the sake of the other's own genuine need to become whole and to grow as a person. In translating Mayeroff's definition of caring to Christian thinking, the aim of caring becomes attending to another so that the other person also is capacitated to function as a person who cares. Growth is not adequately understood as a means of self-actualization but becomes the manner by which a kingdom of caring is extended in the world. Caring begets caring. God's care for us enables our care for one another and for the world. We care for others with God's care so that they too become people who care.

As God's stewards, we are summoned to learn the life of caring. A congregation is a community that fosters caring. Such care begins with respect for oneself. While there is too much talk these days about "doing something just for yourself," one cannot begin to care for others until one is free from preoccupation with one's own needs and energized to attend to the other. The ultimate form of self-care, from a Christian perspective, is trusting in the promise of God's personal love. Unless one's life is rooted in God's unconditional care, the foundation for caring for others is tenuous. This means that self-care not only entails attention to diet, sleep, and sufficient exercise as essential components but also necessarily includes prayer, devotions, and worship. As one is regularly cared for by the Word and Sacrament of God, one receives a centered existence that sets one free to care for others.

The primary laboratory in which one learns the requisites of caring is the family. If one is to acquire the habit of caring, then one must begin with the practices of listening, patience, forbearance, courage, self-sacrifice, trust, and forgiveness as it unfolds in the life of a family. Whether we consider the relationships with parents, siblings, spouse, or children, the intense closeness of a family challenges every idealistic portrait of human community. Family life provides the arena in which the most destructive human behaviors can emerge. And at the same time, families can offer a glimpse of what human community was intended to be. To a large degree, what one learns about caring from one's family of origin serves as the basis for the ability to care in the world beyond one's family. A successful family nurtures persons who are capacitated to move beyond the confines of the family into relationships of care for others.

The circle of care extends into the realms of the congregation, workplace, and local community. The congregation at worship provides the center where one practices the rudiments of caring. The relationships among members of a congregation provide ample opportunity to exercise care, whether through listening, verbal support, or doing a favor. Projects of the congregation offer various outlets where care for those in special need can be organized and executed.

The workplace too is a setting in which one has regular opportunity for rendering care. This takes place initially through the responsible fulfillment of one's duties at work. Luther liked to describe the workplace as the arena through which God upholds the fabric of creation. If one cares, that becomes evident in one's attitude toward one's job. Those who experience a lack of meaningful employment require counseling either to discover ways to renew their sense of purpose or to risk setting out in a new direction. With the precariousness of the current employment situation, many feel trapped in unfulfilling work due to their need for an income. Yet it may be a great tragedy to pour out one's lifeblood in an occupation that one detests solely for the sake of a paycheck rather than risk a change.

The workplace also affords the opportunity to care for the persons with whom one works. A level of collegiality is attained among colleagues at work that affords the possibility of genuine caring. A steward, nurtured in the experience of Christian community in the congregation, has a model for relating to others that goes beyond business as usual. Expressions of solidarity at the joys and sorrows of those one knows at work expand the reach of God's caring in powerful ways.

A steward also sees the wider community as a realm for caring. Schools, civic organizations, charitable causes, and volunteer groups offer possible arenas of service. For some there is the danger of making too many commitments and therefore not being able to do any of them well. For most Christians, however, there is too little thought given to community service as a kind of stewardship. One should even recognize involvement in the political process as an extension of Christian stewardship, as we care collectively for the leadership and direction of our community's common life.

Christian stewardship and caring goes beyond all the circles already mentioned, however, to encompass the entire globe. Issues confronting the nation—health care, criminal justice, domestic violence, immigration policies, and so forth—summon a thoughtful response from Christians who care. Likewise the affairs of other nations raise questions of responsibility for the steward—war, hunger, terrorism, environmental degradation, and so on. In our time it has become extremely urgent to develop conscientious policies of caring for the earth and its endangered ecosystems. Each of these matters we will take up again in remaining chapters.

The congregation, by instilling the mindset of stewardship among its membership and by corporately practicing the art of caring, reinforces a strong sense of Christian identity. The church, composed of its many members, is accountable to God for taking care of the portion assigned to it for flourishing. The idea of stewardship grounds congregational identity in its relationship and responsibility to God above all else. At the same time, the matter of stewardship points the congregation beyond itself to the mission of caring for the earth and all that dwell therein. Within a theology of the congregation, stewardship functions at the juncture between claiming our identity and becoming active in mission.

Worship is the centerpiece of this theology of the congregation. At worship, the congregation rehearses its identity as people of the kingdom. In worship, Word and Sacrament, it encounters the living Lord, who transforms it into the people of God. From worship we are sent into the world in mission.

The four chapters of this section of the book have elaborated the first of two foci in a theology of the congregation. Prayer, education, life in community, and stewardship are indispensable components of a congregation that knows its true identity. Prayer centers us in our relationship with the triune God and teaches us to join Christ's own intercessions on behalf of the world. A congregation immerses itself in the way of Christian discipleship through its educational efforts, following the example of the saints who have gone before. In its communal life, the congregation celebrates the friendship of the crucified Christ through its "life together" (Bonhoeffer) in an egalitarian communion—people and pastor—seeking to incorporate those of every age, ethnicity, and social position. Within the congregation, the people of God learn to see themselves as stewards of all the good gifts God has given them. Tithing and caring, they lead generous lives.

Through worship, prayer, education, life in community, and stewardship, a congregation knows its identity as a people gathered in the name
of Jesus Christ. Whenever a congregation begins to forget the One who
is its origin, it must return to these basic elements. Yet the purpose of
the congregation transcends the formation of its identity. The same Jesus
who calls us together at worship also sends us out to the world in mission. For this reason, we next elaborate the four components that accent
the congregation's essential mission: evangelizing, global connections,
ecumenism, and social ministry. Without these expressions of mission to
others, the vitality of the congregation atrophies and withers.

FOR FURTHER READING

Callahan, Kennon L. *Giving and Stewardship in an Effective Church: A Guide
for Every Member.* San Francisco: Jossey-Bass, 1997.

Durall, Michael. *Creating Congregations of Generous People.* Annapolis Junction, Md.: Alban Institute, 1999.

Fischer, Wallace E. *All Good Gifts: On Doing Biblical Stewardship.* Minneapolis: Augsburg Publishing House, 1979.

Grimm, Eugene. *Generous People: How to Encourage Vital Stewardship.*
Edited by Herb Miller. Nashville: Abingdon, 1992.

Hall, Douglas J. The *Steward: A Biblical Symbol Come to Age.* Eugene, Ore.:
Wipf & Stock, 2004.

Johnson, Douglas W. *The Tithe: Challenge or Legalism?* Nashville: Abingdon, 1989.

McNamara, Patrick H. *More than Money: Portraits of Transformative Stewardship.* Annapolis Junction, Md.: Alban Institute, 1999.

Mayeroff, Milton. *On Caring.* New York: Harper, 1990.

Meeks, M. Douglas. *God the Economist: The Doctrine of God and Political
Economy.* Minneapolis: Fortress Press, 2000.

Mosser, David N. *The Stewardship Companion: Lectionary Resources for Preaching.* Louisville: Westminster John Knox, 2007.

Powell, Mark Allan. *Giving to God: The Bible's Good News about Living a
Generous Life.* Grand Rapids: Eerdmans, 2006.

Williams, Rosemary, with Joanne Kabak. *The Woman's Book of Money and Spiritual Vision: Putting Your Spiritual Values in Financial Practice.* Makawao, Hawaii: Inner Ocean, 2001.

FOR REFLECTION AND DISCUSSION

1. What does it mean to say "God owns everything"? What difference would taking this conviction seriously make in your congregation?
2. How are you captive to the consumer culture in which we live? What steps can your congregation take to help people escape from this bondage?
3. What is stewardship? How can your congregation teach the biblical view that stewardship involves a comprehensive approach to life?
4. What have been some of the key influences shaping your own attitudes toward money? How might tithing be valuable as a spiritual practice in seeking to worship God above all things?
5. What are some of the ways you understand your life as extending God's care to others? How can your congregation assist people to see their daily lives as ministries of Christian care?

PART THREE: MISSION

INTRODUCTION

A holistic theology of the congregation revolves around two poles, identity and mission. In part 2, we examined the ministry of the congregation with an eye toward those functions that most contribute to the formation and nurture of Christian identity: prayer, education, life in community, and stewardship. Already the direction of the discussion has pointed, however, toward the movement of congregational ministry from focus on its identity to outreach in mission. The mission of the congregation (to be addressed in the next four chapters) is also organized under four categories: evangelizing, global connections, ecumenism, and social ministry. Together these dimensions of mission provide direction for a comprehensive vision of congregational interaction with a local community and the world at large.

We might again ask at this juncture: What is the purpose of the Christian congregation? The answer that guides this book is: The purpose of the Christian congregation is to be a mediator of the salvation that God in Jesus Christ is bringing to all people. *Salvation* means God's project of bringing wholeness to human life by restoring us to right relationships—with God, one another, and the creation itself. The gospel of salvation is proclaimed as the forgiveness of sins and the justification of the sinner before God, inviting us into a living relationship with God based on trust. The meaning of salvation, however, transcends individual piety to incorporate the complex web of human relationships with one another and the created world.

Evangelizing focuses on the task of speaking the gospel to others in order that they might be incorporated into the people of God, the church. Salvation becomes personal through the work of congregations that are evangelical.

Global connections establish the breadth of God's salvific concern, a concern that makes relative national boundaries and other divisive distinctions in favor of one, holy, catholic, and apostolic church on earth. This dimension of the congregation's life achieves new importance in an age of mass communication when our mutual interdependence becomes increasingly obvious.

Ecumenism broadens the scope of the congregation's mission to include the restoration of life-giving relationships among Christians, who have been divided into hundreds of denominations and sects. Salvation becomes manifest as estranged Christian groups move toward fellowship at the Lord's Table.

Finally, social ministry—on behalf of the hungry, those threatened by violence, the endangered earth ecosystem—aims to reestablish relationships in accordance with the church's vision of the kingdom of God. The mission of God, in whose service the church ministers, finds its final consummation in the eternity of God's eschatological kingdom. In the meantime, the church properly serves God's salvific purposes by engaging in diverse ministries that aim at the just structuring of power relationships and the resolution of conflict by peaceful means.

The mission of the church (and thereby of the congregation) is not an either/or focus—either on helping individuals or on social problems. Rather, the salvation of God integrally incorporates both dimensions. A congregation's mission is diminished to the degree that it fails to include in some measure all four dimensions now to be elaborated.

Chapter Nine

Evangelizing:
Speaking the Kingdom

The doctrine of the Trinity is not an easy topic to teach or preach. Often, explicit references to the Trinity are relegated to the one Sunday in the church year devoted to this theme. Preachers may attempt to describe the Trinity on this occasion with reference to conventional analogies, for example, how water can take three forms: liquid, solid, or gas. Never mind that such an analogy points toward one of the most common trinitarian heresies, modalism! Whenever we first consider the Trinity as a mathematical dilemma that needs to be explained, we have already lost the essence of its truth.

The Holy Trinity is not a mathematical improbability. Rather, it is the Christian affirmation about the character of God. The Trinity gives expression to the Christian understanding that *God by nature is a God in mission.* The First Person of the Trinity, the Father, did not choose to remain isolated in divine grandeur forever, basking in the wonder of glory. Instead, God decided to create a world to be the recipient of divine pleasure and love. God took the risk of creating a universe and this earth, populating it with amazing creatures, including one creature made in God's own image. God created the world as an act of mission, in order for there to exist recipients of divine love.

The Second Person of the Trinity, the Son, became incarnate in human flesh in order to carry out the divine mission of reconciliation. As human beings deviated from God's intended purposes, God did not choose simply to abandon them. Rather, God imagined a daring act of rescue in order to return them to life-giving relationship: "I will become one of them." In Jesus' proclamation and embodiment of the kingdom, by his cross, and in the power of the resurrection, God revealed inexhaustible mercy and kindness to humankind. Jesus came to seek and to save sinners. Jesus invited them and invites us to know the forgiveness and grace of God's goodness. God sent Jesus Christ into the world as a bold initiative in divine mission.

The Third Person of the Trinity, the Holy Spirit, reveals the relentlessness of God in seeking and saving what has become estranged. The Holy Spirit is the power of God to sustain and preserve the creation moment in and moment out. The Holy Spirit is the energy of God expended to restore what has become alienated back into life-giving relationship with God. The Holy Spirit is the animated presence of God in the world to accomplish *shalom*, the restoration of all things to their created purpose: God in relationship with humans, humans in relationship with one another, and all things in harmonious relationship both with God and with humanity. The Holy Spirit works explicitly in Word and Sacrament, the material of the liturgy, and works implicitly in all of life to accomplish God's ultimate mission of bringing the kingdom in its fullness.

In this chapter, we explore one particular dimension of God's mission, the sending of the church into the work of evangelizing. The remaining chapters of part 3 will reflect on other aspects of God's mission through the church: global connections, ecumenism, and social ministry. We begin with this question: What does it mean to do the work of evangelist in our times?

Unprecedented Diversity: Are We Ready to Be Changed?

For centuries, the church in North America could depend on two reliable methods of church growth: immigration and propagation. For several generations, a ready-made mission field kept arriving by the boatload from Europe in the persons of European immigrants. These immigrants had urgent need of the church's ministry as they searched for familiar grounding in a new land. In the church, they gathered with others who shared their language and culture and religious faith. The church served as a haven for those adrift in the sea change of the new world.

At the same time, the church was assured of growth as these immigrants grew their own families. Children were brought for baptism in their ethnic congregations and grew up in the borderland between the culture of their parents and the larger American culture. Through the 1950s, these two methods of outreach continued to suffice. The churches were sustained by the homogeneity of their European heritage and the baby boom following the Second World War.

All of this has changed in the last fifty years. No longer is the future of congregations assured by European immigration and propagation. In case we have not noticed, there are still many immigrants arriving in North America. But they are no longer arriving in large numbers from northern Europe. Likewise, the future of the congregation is in no way guaranteed by the baptizing of our own children. The new generations know no brand loyalty. If they eventually join a church (which is itself no sure thing), they are more than likely to do so after shopping around to select the product that "feels right" and "meets their needs" in the best way.

Moreover, there are dramatic cultural changes at work that jeopardize the future of many congregations. We live in a time and country characterized by unprecedented diversity. Diana Eck has documented how the United States has become the most culturally and religiously diverse nation in the history of the world.

Beginning with the immigration legislation of 1965, large numbers of immigrants began to arrive in the U.S. from countries in Asia, Africa, and Latin America who bring a breadth of cultural diversity once unimaginable in "WASP" America (white Anglo-Saxon Protestant). Beyond the tide of legal immigration, political instability and economic uncertainty have generated huge numbers of other immigrants, especially from the Spanish-speaking countries of Central and South America. Spanish is rapidly becoming the second language of the

United States. And the Christian church has not begun to keep up with these cultural changes.

Not only are we surrounded with unprecedented cultural diversity, we are also facing a much more complex interreligious context for Christian mission in the U.S. Because those who immigrate bring their religious faith with them, there are dramatic shifts in religious allegiance that the church may be ill prepared to negotiate. For example, there are now more Muslims in the U.S. than either Episcopalians or Presbyterians. How do we learn to articulate the hope that is in us (1 Pet 3:15) in relationship to representatives of all the world's great religions living in our midst?

As we have discussed in chapter 6, we also inhabit a culture that is clearly post-Christian. We can no longer depend on cultural supports to make Christians for us. There was a day when we could assume young people would be familiar with biblical figures and church holidays merely by growing up in this national culture. However, we can no longer make that assumption. Even the most central biblical personages—Moses, David, Mary, or Paul—are no longer familiar in the larger culture. Likewise, we can no longer assume that people will naturally know that Christmas or Easter have anything to do with the life of Jesus. If anything, they will only know Christmas as a consumer festival and Easter as a day for coloring eggs and enjoying the arrival of spring.

If Christian congregations are going to make the gospel known to the world, they will need to operate with intentionality about Christian formation and evangelizing that they have never before practiced. This involves both focused "in reach" to our present constituencies, raising children to claim their identity as disciples of Jesus, and "outreach" to new populations, especially to those recent immigrants who are now living as neighbors in our communities.

Congregations need to develop new and deliberate strategies of outreach, for example, in serving their Spanish-speaking neighbors. There are several different approaches that require different levels of commitment. One strategy is to offer social services to assist immigrants in addressing basic human needs. Another is to organize English as a second language classes to meet at the church. Another is to open up the use of one's church building for use by a Spanish-speaking congregation, arranging the schedules to accommodate both congregations. Another would be to begin a satellite of one's congregation at another site for Spanish-language worship and congregational life. Yet another level of challenge would involve trying to invite Spanish speakers to join one's own congregation. This last proposal requires a high degree of cultural literacy and language fluency, far more than we may begin to imagine.

In all congregational efforts to reach out to new people, especially to new ethnic populations, we need to keep one central question in mind: *Are we ready to be changed?* Often, we imagine our congregation is a "friendly" place. By this we may unwittingly assume that all people are equally welcome. However, closer examination may disclose that what we really mean is something like this: If you become like us, then you will be welcome. What we really expect is that the newcomer will change to conform to our own image: Once you adapt to our (implicit) expectations and become "one of us," then you will be welcome.

Instead of operating with this unspoken and insidious assumption, congregations will only become truly welcoming when they themselves are *ready to be changed* by others. Instead of expecting others to fit in, we need to become interested in and excited by the new gifts that different people bring into our midst. How can we truly celebrate the gifts others will inevitably bring? How can we become truly ready to be changed by the arrival of those who neither look nor think like us? Until we truly are ready to learn the art of hospitality, the welcome of the stranger, our efforts at evangelizing will be compromised.

Evangelizing Defined

Paul Rajashekar quips that there is only one great commission that mainline congregations have ever obeyed. This is the commission given by Jesus to the healed leper in Mark 1:44: "See that you say nothing to anyone"! In one study, a major Protestant denomination examined how often its members on the average invited another person to attend worship. The finding: once every twenty-two years!

We have come to consider evangelism as something difficult and complicated. For this reason, we relegate the task of evangelism to the hired and trained professional, the pastor. Or we relegate the work of evangelism to those willing to serve on the congregation's evangelism committee, usually a very small group. Or we undertake evangelism as a periodic program on the part of the congregation. In order to prepare ourselves for such an emphasis, we often hold a class on evangelism. For four or six weeks we gather in the classroom to review and study the meaning of evangelism. We may even experiment with the practice of evangelism by conversing with other class members. But then we can all breathe a sigh of relief that the class comes to an end. And with the conclusion of the class, so do our efforts at evangelism!

Congregations have come to define evangelism rather broadly. In fact, anything that has to do with publicity has come to be included under the evangelism umbrella. In this way, yellow pages ads, billboards, bumper stickers, refrigerator magnets, web pages, and brochures about the congregation all qualify as evangelism.

The New Testament, however, is much more specific about what constitutes evangelism. The Greek words *euangelion* (noun) and *euangelizō* (verb) refer very precisely to the specific practice of proclaiming the good news to another. Evangelism thus is not a term that encompasses a wide range of practices. Rather, it has to do with speaking the faith to another. It has to do with oral communication, one beggar telling another beggar where to find bread.

The work of an evangelist involves two distinguishable but interrelated practices: evangelical listening and speaking the faith. Evangelical listening means paying close attention to what others say to us, both through their words and through their emotions. Evangelical listening involves remaining alert for the "God question" that underlies what is being shared. It means listening for the human longings, disappointments, fears, dreams, and hopes that in due time need to be connected to the larger horizon of God's comfort and God's promises.

Evangelical listening involves honoring other people by taking them with utmost seriousness as we converse with them. It means listening carefully, listening actively, making sure we have genuinely understood what they are saying. We are not to jump too quickly to giving answers or advice. Rather, we are to ponder deeply what we have heard in order to honor the other by also responding from the depths of our own experience.

The second distinct practice is that of speaking the faith. While we are generally ready to share other kinds of good news that we have experienced, for example, the arrival of a child, the purchase of a new car, or the discovery of an excellent movie or book, we remain reticent about sharing our faith in Jesus. Evangelizing involves learning to speak the faith in ways that correspond to the story we have heard by our listening to others. We will explore more on the art of speaking the faith in the last section of this chapter.

Because of the need to define very exactly the nature of evangelism, the authors of *The Evangelizing Church* have proposed that we stop thinking of evangelism as an "ism." This means the church must stop imagining evangelism as just another compartment of congregational life, something undertaken by a single committee or as a periodic program of some kind. Instead, we need to reclaim "evangelizing" as a core dimension of what it means to be a Christian person and a Christian congregation. If "evangelism" describes the compartmentalization of the evangelical calling, then let "evangelizing" refer to the sharing of the faith as an indispensable dimension of all we are and do as Christian persons and Christian congregations. Either we are an evangelizing church or we are no church at all.

There are three major obstacles that impede our journey to becoming an evangelizing church. First, we have never actualized the promise of the Reformation regarding the ministry of all the baptized. Instead, we have over the centuries created an elaborate dependency system in which the baptized are overly reliant on the leadership of pastors. This state of affairs is known as clericalism. While pastors have a particular gift and ministry among the baptized, the stewardship of Word and Sacrament, the laity are regularly disempowered from claiming and sharing their own gifts in the ministry of the church. Clericalism is fed both by the "need to be needed" on the part of pastors and by the feigned incompetence on the part of church members. In many places, we have achieved a comfortable homeostasis that fosters the continuation of the clerical dependency system. How do we recover the truth of the priesthood of all believers, the ministry of all the baptized? One of the key areas is evangelizing, equipping the baptized to speak the faith to others.

A second formidable obstacle is the privatization of the faith in the modern world. Since the nineteenth century, religion has been more and more relegated to the private realm and excluded from the public square. Religion came to be understood as a personal matter, not something one talks about in polite company. On the one hand, the privatization of religious faith has contributed something essential to peaceful coexistence among those who hold diverse religious viewpoints: tolerance. Being tolerant of others is indeed a civic virtue necessary for pluralistic society. But the price of tolerance has been relegation of faith to a matter of personal preference. In this way, faith has become increasingly individualized and thereby marginalized as a social force. The privatization of faith contradicts the character of the Christian gospel with its universal truth claims. How do we learn to remain conscientiously respectful of others, even while we boldly speak the truth of the gospel of Jesus Christ? This is a major challenge facing the evangelizing church in our time.

Third, we remain all too captive to the idolatry of our own ethnicity. Because many of our congregations originated as ethnic enclaves, it is difficult for us to distinguish between our own ethnic traditions and the essence of the Christian faith, which transcends particular ethnic identities. In many congregations, there is scarcely awareness about how the focus on a single ethnic identity implicitly excludes those who do not share that tradition. The jokes we tell and the festivals we organize can unwittingly marginalize many people from our congregational life. God seeks to be known in every ethnic tradition. We are called to celebrate every ethnic tradition as a vehicle for God's presence. Can we learn how to celebrate a range of ethnic heritages and thereby avoid exclusionary focus on our own? We must become intentionally multicultural in our congregational life, fluent in a variety of cultural expressions, including the one that distinguished the congregation at its origins.

Becoming an evangelizing church entails facing these obstacles directly and growing in our capacity to live and speak the faith to others.

We must claim the gifts of all the baptized, affirm the need to make public witness to the Christian gospel, and embrace God's blessing on ethnicities not our own. We remain faithful to the great commission in our time by recovering the core meaning of evangelizing as proclaiming the faith to the world.

Learning to Speak the Faith

The church in the twenty-first century stands at a crossroads. Either we learn what it means to become an evangelizing church or we will give way to other traditions that know better then we how to navigate the contemporary religious landscape. The church of Christendom must undergo a dramatic culture change if it is to ready itself to enter the post-Christian religious marketplace of the coming decades. Culture change does not happen automatically or easily. However, there are defined practices that can be implemented to serve as catalysts for the culture change needed in becoming an evangelizing congregation.

In learning to speak the faith, four practices can contribute to changing the culture of the congregation. First, leaders need to learn to *model* speaking the faith to others. This does not refer to speaking the faith in the formal settings at worship or in preaching and teaching. It means learning to speak the faith conversationally as a natural aspect of daily living. Those who are leaders in the church, pastors as well as lay leaders, experience the presence of God as part of their life journey. We interpret the events of our lives in relationship to God's story and look for God's hand in guiding what unfolds. Church leaders need to become comfortable making explicit references to the activity of God and Jesus Christ as they interpret to others the difference God in Christ makes in their lives. Such modeling can have a transforming effect on how others begin to interpret and articulate their own life journey.

Second, *small groups* need to be organized for the intentional purpose of learning to speak about our daily lives in relationship to God's activity. There are already many small groups in congregational life. Some of these already encourage the practice of speaking one's faith to others (for example, women's circles or prayer groups). But there is an opportunity for encouraging the formation of additional small groups in the congregation with the express purpose of learning to pray together and read the Bible in relationship to the opportunities and challenges of living a Christian life day by day. Such groups are led by laypersons who are coached in the basics of group dynamics. The agenda for such groups is very clear: to speak and pray together about the involvement of God in daily life.

Third, there is great formation in the *mentoring* of those new to the Christian way by those with rich experiences to share. We are talking here about a particular kind of mentoring relationship. The mentor needs to be prepared and trained to focus particularly on the integration of faith and life. Mentors need to be ready to share the story of their own faith journey with those who are mentored. They need to be ready to describe the intersection between their Christian faith and the struggles they are facing in their own lives. Such mentoring involves speaking the faith in a trusted relationship with a young person or with new members of the congregation.

Fourth, we need to nurture and develop the practice of *testimony at worship*. The Service of the Word can be expanded from the reading of Scripture lessons and the proclamation of the sermon to include the witness of Christians to the activity of God experienced in their lives. Such testimony has been a regular component in stewardship campaigns, because those trained in sales know the power of personal witnessing. How much more the transformative effect on congregational culture to have members regularly offer public testimony to God's presence in their lives as part of the worship service! Pastors need to be prepared to accompany members in learning the art of testimony, encouraging and guiding them in the process. This particular practice, even if introduced quarterly or monthly, has tremendous potential to nurture the speaking of the faith as a dimension of congregational culture.

Paul writes: "But how are they to call on one in whom they have not believed? And how are they to believe in one of whom they have never heard? And how are they to hear without someone to proclaim him? And how are they to proclaim him unless they are sent? As it is written, 'How beautiful are the feet of those who bring good news!' But not all have obeyed the good news; for Isaiah says, 'Lord, who has believed our message?' So faith comes from what is heard, and what is heard comes through the word of Christ" (Rom 10:14-17). Fulfilling the great commission (Matt 28:19-20) requires our learning to speak the faith to others.

What is the quality of the speech that can serve God's mission through the outreach of an evangelizing congregation? Evangelizing speech must be based on one's own genuine life experience. We speak best about what we have come to know in the ups and downs of our own biography. It must be grounded in our own existential journey.

Evangelizing speech must also be explicit, naming God and Jesus Christ as active participants in one's own life. It is important that we not shy away from testifying directly to the difference that God in Christ has made in the living of our lives. Especially in this post-Christian culture, we must be bold in resisting the cultural pressure to privatize the faith.

Evangelizing speech must also be contextual, based on careful listening to what has been said by the one with whom we speak. Evangelical listening is a prerequisite for our own speaking the faith to others. We must carefully correlate between what we have heard and the story we have to share. This means spontaneity in our speaking, not relying on static formulas.

Finally, evangelizing speech is authentic. This means there is a vital correspondence between the words we speak and how we live our lives. Words are rendered empty by hypocrisy. This does not mean that we who speak are without sin. But it does mean that we are engaged in a struggle to live with integrity, even when we fall short of our ideals.

The strong emphasis on speaking the faith as the work of an evangelist in this chapter will be complemented by the themes of the remaining chapters. The mission of the congregation is made whole as we build global connections, engage in ecumenical partnerships, and take initiative in social ministry. The identity of the church, which is funded by worship, prayer, education, life in community, and stewardship comes to expression in mission through these core activities. Evangelizing articulates what God has to do with the whole as well as each of the parts.

FOR FURTHER READING

Bliese, Richard H., and Craig Van Gelder, eds. *The Evangelizing Church: A Lutheran Contribution.* Minneapolis: Augsburg Fortress, 2005.

Bowen, John P. *Evangelism for Normal People.* Minneapolis: Augsburg Fortress, 2002.

Fryer, Kelly A. *Reclaiming the "E" Word: Waking Up to Our Evangelical Identity.* Minneapolis: Augsburg Fortress, 2008.

Heath, Elaine A. *The Mystic Way of Evangelism: A Contemplative Vision for Christian Outreach.* Grand Rapids: Baker Academic, 2008.

Hunter, George G., III. *The Celtic Way of Evangelism: How Christianity Can Reach the West . . . Again.* Nashville: Abingdon, 2000.

Kallenberg, Brad J. *Live to Tell: Evangelism for a Postmodern Age.* Grand Rapids: Brazos, 2002.

Linn, Jan. *Reclaiming Evangelism: A Practical Guide for Mainline Churches.* St. Louis: Chalice, 1998.

Quere, Ralph W. *Evangelical Witness: The Message, Medium, Mission, and Method of Evangelism.* Minneapolis: Augsburg, 1975.

Roxburgh, Alan J., and Fred Romanuk. *The Missional Leader: Equipping Your Church to Reach a Changing World.* San Francisco: Jossey-Bass, 2006.

Stone, Bryan P. *Evangelism after Christendom: The Theology and Practice of Christian Witness.* Grand Rapids: Brazos, 2007.

Thomsen, Mark W. *Jesus, the Word, and the Way of the Cross: An Engagement with Muslims, Buddhists, and Other Peoples of Faith.* Minneapolis: Lutheran University Press, 2008.

Van Gelder, Craig. *The Ministry of the Missional Church: A Community Led by the Spirit.* Grand Rapids: Baker, 2007.

FOR REFLECTION AND DISCUSSION

1. How does the Trinity express the character of God as missionary? How can we better understand the Trinity by seeing it in terms of God's essential missionary activity?

2. What signs do you see of increasing cultural and religious diversity in the community where you live? What can you do to reach out to the new people who are living in your community, especially to those who are different from you?

3. Are you ready to be changed by the gifts new people will inevitably bring to your congregation? How can you ready yourself for embracing the changes that the inclusion of new people will provoke?

4. When has someone else spoken to you about their Christian faith? What impact did that speaking have on your own life and faith?

5. How is speaking the faith an important part of your congregational culture? What practices might you introduce to nurture the speaking of the faith as a core dimension of your congregation's identity and mission?

Chapter Ten

Global Connections: The Church Catholic

"We believe in one holy catholic and apostolic church."

The church has confessed this faith since the fourth century, in the formula of the Nicene Creed. Following the Reformation and the ensuing polemic between Protestants and Roman Catholics, many Protestant groups changed the translation of the word *catholic* to *Christian*. While an understandable change given the animosity generated over centuries of mistrust, we can rejoice that the interconfessional climate has improved to the point where we can reclaim the use of the original word and its original meaning. *Catholic* means universal. We confess at worship through this creed that God rules over one, single, universal church, a church undivided over time and space. Throughout history and still today throughout the world, in God's eyes there exists only one catholic church.

Clearly, this is a confession of faith, not a statement based on empirical evidence. The church of Jesus Christ appears splintered into fragments based on nationality, language, ethnicity, and many other characteristics. Yet, as we confess in this creed, what divides us does not constitute the essence of the church God intends. Rather, as there is only one Lord, one faith, and one baptism (Eph 4:5), so there is in reality only one catholic church. The one chief obstacle to this confession is that we do not act as though it were true.

Christian congregations are called by the Holy Spirit to live in the reality of the one catholic church that we confess. There are numerous ways that congregations can express their connectedness to Christians and churches in other parts of the world. This chapter explores the possibility that every congregation should develop global connections that give expression to the breadth of the faith we confess. Christians in other parts of the world desperately need Christians in the United States to subordinate the rhetoric of nationalism to the unity we share in Christ. By baptism, we have been formed into one body. When our brothers and sisters on other continents are in pain, we too suffer with them. Likewise, when they rejoice, we receive great blessings. "For the peace of the whole world, for the well-being of the people of God, and for the unity of all, let us pray to the Lord" (*Kyrie*).

Centrifugal Force of the Gospel

The catholicity of the church of Jesus Christ came clearly to expression already on Pentecost, the church's birthday. The Holy Spirit in wind and flame united in faith those whose languages and nationalities otherwise would serve to divide. Each one heard the others speaking in the native language of each (Acts 2:6). While skeptics sneered, the Holy Spirit revealed the catholicity of the church that shattered the barriers of language, ethnicity, and nationality conventionally used to carve up humanity. The Holy Spirit enlivened human understanding to unite all those gathered into the one catholic church of Jesus Christ.

The spirit of Pentecost propelled the apostles outward. The gospel of the resurrected Jesus exhibits a centrifugal force that thrust these members of the earliest church into a universal mission. Though Jews by birth and circumcision, the apostles were entrusted with the commission to baptize all who repented and believed the good news. Not without agony did the church in Jerusalem concede that Gentiles be admitted as equal partners in the church without the necessity of submitting to at least some provisions of the law. As Acts of the Apostles tells the story, however, under the persistent challenge of Paul and the persuasion of the Spirit over Peter, Gentiles came to belong to the church of Jesus Christ by their confession of faith alone. This was a dramatic change of course that continues to have radical implications for the life of the church today.

In the early decades after the resurrection, the gospel of Jesus Christ spread with amazing celerity. Using the privilege of Roman citizenship and his upbringing as a Pharisee, Paul took the gospel first to Jews and then to Gentiles throughout the southern reaches of the Roman Empire. Soon there were followers of the Way of Jesus Christ not only in Palestine and Syria but also in Cappadocia, Galatia, Asia Minor, Macedonia, and even Rome itself. The widespread experience of persecution and even martyrdom demonstrates that these early Christians understood the catholicity of the church. Many willingly suffered humiliation and death rather than submit to the machinations of an empire requiring them to confess the divinity of Caesar. The blood of the martyrs bound the followers of Jesus in a community that transcended all other allegiances.

The Romanization of the church, set in motion when Constantine bestowed favored status upon the church beginning in the fourth century, gave new meaning to the word *catholic*. As the empire convulsed to the breaking point, one political aim of the emperor was to employ Christianity as an adhesive to bind together what was tearing apart. The formulation of the Nicene Creed itself was influenced by these developments, as the political order looked to the church to provide a basis for unity. This led to the development of what we now call "Christendom," outlined in chapter 6, which in many ways came to compromise the integrity of Christian conviction.

At the same time, the Constantinian arrangement gave the church institutional privileges for spreading the word about Jesus to the farthest reaches of Rome's influence. During the Holy Roman Empire, converts to Jesus from the British Isles in the fifth, sixth, and seventh centuries took the gospel into the remainder of western Europe. From 800 to 1300, the process of Christianization spread northward into Scandinavia and eastward across eastern Europe. In the years after 1400, Christian mission extended itself ever farther eastward, toward Asia.

The close connection between baptism and citizenship in the church of the Middle Ages was a blessing for facilitating access to new territory but a curse in terms of compromising the content of the faith. The significance of baptism as that which constitutes the catholicity of the church became subordinated to the exigencies of good citizenship. This confusion about Christian identity is nowhere more manifest than in the struggles of the Reformation of the sixteenth century. What constitutes true Christianity? Submitting to the dictates of the Holy Roman Emperor? Submitting to the decrees of the Holy Roman Pope? Or submitting to the lordship of Jesus Christ as revealed in Holy Scripture? The Reformation gave the occasion for decoupling baptism from citizenship. Ironically, this moment of opportunity gave rise not so much to a greater loyalty to Jesus Christ that transcended the boundaries dividing countries but rather to a new and more avid territorialism. Churches became ever more closely identified with political rule under the provisions of the Peace of Westphalia (1648), whereby the religion of the territorial ruler determined the favored religion of the territory.

During the age of European expansion, Christianity spread through missionary efforts and immigration to both North and South America. Tragically, this was a period in which the gospel message was all too regularly used as an imperialistic weapon, lending deep ambiguity to the evangelization process. The nineteenth century saw the apex of organized missionary activity to Africa and Asia. Again, a tragic dimension characterized this period, as the Christian gospel was too narrowly identified with Western culture. It has only been in recent decades that the church has begun to intentionally divest the Christian message of its cultural biases in order to think Christian truth with integrity in ways indigenous to host cultures.

This cursory survey of the globalization of Christianity aims to demonstrate that the thrust of the gospel is inherently inclusive of all people on earth, regardless of language, ethnicity, or nationality. Unlike most other world religions (with the exception of Islam), Christianity is inherently a missionary religion that aims at unifying all humankind through faith in Christ Jesus. Baptism is no respecter of human distinctions but theologically functions as the means for creating a new community, uniting persons in the body of Christ as a form of community that subordinates all other allegiances. Jesus Christ died for all. And so by faith in Jesus Christ, all are joined into a new fellowship that makes relative all other human bonds. Under the parenthood of God, Jesus taught that all his followers are sisters and brothers. We speak blithely of the church as a family. But are we convinced that this is something more than mere sentimentalism? Is the bond in Christ, which unites people of different ethnicities, languages, and nationalities, really more powerful than any other identification? The economic and political commitments of many Christians seem to belie such claims.

The eschatological vision of the Christian faith is one of a community in which all people are united in praise of Jesus Christ: "After this I looked, and there was a great multitude that no one could count, from every nation, from all tribes and peoples and languages, standing before the throne and before the Lamb, robed in white, with palm branches in their hands. They cried out in a loud voice, saying, 'Salvation belongs to our God who is seated on the throne, and to the Lamb!'" (Rev 7:9-10). The gospel of Jesus Christ propels its witnesses into the entire world with the mission of uniting all people by faith in this name. The failure of the church to fulfill this calling in no way negates the truth of the theological claim.

Beyond Nationalism

The age of the Enlightenment brought into existence a revolutionary new form of human organization, the nation-state. In opposition to all forms of traditional authoritarianism, nations were to be ordered not by privileged classes who assume power according to wealth, property, or heredity, but by a contract between those governed and those who govern. By definition, a nation-state is a nation whose principle of organization is not language, tribe, or ethnicity but a contractual agreement among those who live there, that is, a state. Enlightenment thinkers sought to cast off Bible, pope, and king insofar as they restricted the free reign of human reason to structure human affairs.

Political theorists such as John Locke argued for government to be established according to the mutual consent of the governed, with laws defined in constitutions limiting the power of those who rule. Nations were to be organized according to a reasoned agreement that defends the individual's rights to life, liberty, and property. The French and American Revolutions gave birth to the models for all subsequent Western-style democracies. A nation came to be characterized by a constitution, bill of rights, the participation of an electorate, and a system of representative government (legislative, judicial, and executive branches).

Such an organization overcame many deficits of the ancient feudal system, securing rights for many who lacked them under previous systems of governance. For women and people of color, claiming these rights has meant a long and arduous struggle. Citizens who are governed under a system of law have avenues of recourse in changing current or advocating new legislation. They are to be afforded due process in defending themselves from accusations. Political and civil rights are protected by the authority of the state—for example, the freedoms of speech, assembly, or religion. The nation-state introduced a revolutionary new concept in contrast to traditional, hierarchical forms of political governance. The achievements of the democratic model in ordering human affairs, and especially in establishing checks and balances on the abuse of power, should not be undervalued.

In the realm of international affairs, however, the last two centuries have seen the steady emergence of the nation-state as the highest arbiter of global power. Even where adequate constitutional structures are lacking within a particular nation, the sovereignty of that nation-state in pursuing policies on behalf of its own self-interest has developed into the standing dogma in international relationships. For the citizen of the nation-state, patriotism has come to entail unquestioning loyalty to the international policies of one's own nation insofar as these claim to involve national security.

In the United States, the identity of the nation-state has been powerfully shaped by an unofficial, though all-pervasive, civil religion. Civil religion in the United States is exercised through myths and rituals that provide a "sacred canopy" over all affairs of state (Peter Berger). The Pledge of Allegiance declares the United States as "one nation under God," and the nation's currency bears the imprint "in God we trust." National holidays, such as Independence Day, Memorial Day, or Thanksgiving, are celebrated with many trappings of religious observance. Belief in God has become inextricably intertwined with loyalty to the nation.

The greatest dilemma posed to Christian faith by the nation-state and its civil religion is an idolatrous claim for what is ultimate. This is seen particularly in the arena of international relationships. The nation-state exacts a high price from those who resist its established policies, particularly (though not exclusively) in times of war. We need think only of the crisis of conscience faced by Dietrich Bonhoeffer during the church struggle in Nazi Germany. Bonhoeffer and the church in Germany faced the mutually exclusive choice: either loyalty to the nation or loyalty to Jesus Christ. Nations always operate with the conviction that their policies have divine authorization.

While an exacting treatment of the ethics of international affairs is beyond the scope of this book, we focus our attention on one particular aspect of international relations with pointed implications for those who share the Christian faith. This is not to suggest Christians are unconcerned about matters of universal human justice. More will be said about that in the chapter on social ministry. We refer here to the particular situation when one nation's policies have devastating consequences for people in another nation, especially for those who share the same Christian faith. In this case there arises an acute dilemma for the Christian conscience. Does my ultimate loyalty go to my nation, with its claim to divine sanction or does my loyalty belong to my brothers and sisters in the one body of Christ, even though they are citizens of an enemy nation?

The theological claim, based on the confession of faith in the catholicity of the church, is that the greater loyalty is to those who share one common baptism. The consequences of such a conviction are manifold. The claim to ultimacy by the state must be relativized. National policies that endanger the well-being of brothers and sisters in Christ must be scrutinized and questioned. Civil disobedience is warranted where national hubris violates the safety of those "foreigners" who belong to the one body of Christ. Not only is the water of baptism thicker than the blood of kinship, but citizenship in the kingdom of God demands higher allegiance than that pledged to the flag.

The threat of idolatry that comes from the nation-state is one of the gravest challenges facing the contemporary church. To dissent from the identification of God and country is to commit an act of heresy. Yet loyalty to Jesus Christ means we take as seriously as the early church that discipleship of Jesus in the fellowship of the church takes precedence over our allegiance to Caesar. The most serious dilemmas facing the future of our earth—starvation, homelessness, disease, war, militarization, nuclear proliferation, environmental degradation—each remain unsolvable insofar as nation-states establish their own privilege as arbiters of the highest good.

Christian people are needed to serve as leaven for thinking in terms larger than national self-interest and doing so for the theological reason that the church of Jesus Christ transcends all national boundaries. If we are to address the problems that summon our most urgent attention, we must increasingly recognize our global connectedness and do so beginning with the household of faith.

Global Connections in the Congregation

To assert that the nation-state deserves only our penultimate allegiance is to teach an unconventional and subversive wisdom. Yet this is what a congregation affirms with every confession of the Nicene Creed. The history of the church and the story of the spread of the gospel instruct us in the global dimensions of Christian community. Christian congregations have the responsibility—and the ready opportunity—to broaden their vision and deepen their commitment to the catholicity of Christ's church.

The historic liturgy itself grounds one profoundly in the church catholic. To employ ancient words of Scripture from places named Sinai, Galilee, Jerusalem, and Patmos establishes connections with saints in distant locations. To pray traditional litanies, confess historic creeds, and chant ancient benedictions is to connect with all those throughout the world who over the centuries have joined in praising God with a single voice. To worship according to these liturgical forms is a powerful reminder of the catholicity of Christ's church. Not only do we connect ourselves with Christians in distant places from centuries past, but we express our unity with the whole catholic church throughout the world today, as they too participate in worshiping God through these forms.

There are numerous ways to accent the congregation's global connections through liturgical celebration. Intercessions can be offered on a regular basis for the needs of the church in other parts of the world—especially concern for the needs of the hungry, those affected by violence, victims of natural disasters, or in response to other moments of crisis. Another very direct way of establishing a global link is by the selection of music. Given a willingness to learn new things, a congregation's worship can be enhanced by the use of musical settings of the liturgy originating from other cultures. Such ventures require thorough preparation. But there is great richness in discovering expressions of praise deriving from other tongues.

A less dramatic innovation is the introduction of hymns and songs into the liturgy from the church in other parts of the world. These can be matched to the liturgical season and lectionary readings and introduced with reference to the significance of the song in its home country. The use of global music can be further enriched by the use of instrumentation fitting its original context. The images of God and Christ in such hymns and the images used to express the faith expand our own horizons in imagining ways we can more fully honor our God.

The use of artwork and the decor around the church building can contribute to global awareness. Pieces of art from churches in other parts of the world can be borrowed from those who own them or can be exchanged by mail. These can be displayed in a sanctuary or narthex and become a focal point for prayers offered on behalf of the church in that place. From time to time, new items can be introduced. Paraments and banners can serve as vehicles for connecting with Christians in other parts of the world. A map of the world can be hung up in a prominent place and used to speak of missionary efforts or dilemmas faced by the church in other countries.

A congregation seeking to broaden its global connections can invite missionaries home from their assignments to come, teach, and preach about their experiences of the church in the places they have labored. Children and youth benefit greatly from exposure to the global mission of the church. Where it is not already an annual congregational tradition, a "mission festival" can be organized, highlighting, at least for a Sunday or a season, the ministry of the church in a particular place, perhaps with a different focus every year. Seminaries or colleges may be able to provide lists of guest professors or international students who can be invited to make presentations as part of such a mission emphasis. Many local communities have representatives of other cultures already living in their midst who can be resources of information about the church in other parts of the world.

Representatives of congregations can also have their global awareness stretched by attending events held on a regional basis. Some denominations hold global mission events. Synod gatherings frequently include greetings, sermons, and lectures by partners from international churches. Those who attend such meetings can be given the opportunity to share with the entire congregation what they have learned about the challenges and accomplishments of the church's ministry in other contexts.

Members of the congregation who travel as tourists to other parts of the globe can be encouraged to make contact with Christians in the places where they visit in order to build up the vitality of the whole body of Christ. These relationships can become valuable sources of information about the needs of the church in other countries. Perhaps regular correspondence might even develop. One of the most amazing gifts of our catholic faith is the way relationships are freely developed with strangers from other peoples and nations as soon as one discovers that both share a common faith in Jesus Christ.

A more exacting involvement on the part of a congregation is to enter into mission support or mission partnership with a specific church in another part of the world. Denominations are ready resources for assisting congregations to identify projects worthy of their investment and can help establish contact. While the level of commitment required of mission partners is greater than with the other ideas already mentioned, the level of satisfaction can be greater as well. The ongoing contact with a partner church and the relationships that develop among Christians who share each others' faith is an incomparable blessing. Often, such partnerships eventually lead to mutual visits by representatives of the respective communities.

These are but examples of the ways a local congregation can explore its global connections within the one catholic church. A global vision helps bring our practice into conformity with our confession of faith in the catholicity of Christ's church. Moreover, our own faith and ministry are enhanced by the gifts Christians in other parts of the world have to offer to us. For one, as we discover how the Christian gospel is being contextualized in other cultures, we learn how we can better contextualize mission in our own particular setting.

Not least of all, Christians in other parts of the world need our prayers, encouragement, and material support. The disparity of material blessings among the peoples and nations across the globe remains one of the greatest scandals of the modern world. Christians, related by baptism with brothers and sisters on other continents, can be advocates for a humane foreign policy on the part of government. By virtue of our relatedness to people in other parts of the world, the church of Jesus Christ can be a voice for diplomacy and peaceful resolution of conflict in a world where nations too readily resort to violence in attempting to settle their differences. While the scale of a congregation's involvement in making global connections must be appropriate to local circumstances, every congregation can be enriched by intentionally developing the global dimension of the church's confession of faith.

FOR FURTHER READING

Bednarowski, Mary Farrell, ed. *Twentieth-Century Global Christianity: A People's History of Christianity.* Minneapolis: Fortress Press, 2008.

Bosch, David J. *Witness to the World: The Christian Mission in Theological Perspective.* Eugene, Ore.: Wipf & Stock, 2006.

Brown, Robert McAfee, ed. *Kairos: Three Prophetic Challenges to the Church.* Grand Rapids: Eerdmans, 1990.

Foster, Charles R. *Embracing Diversity: Leadership in Multicultural Congregations*. Herndon, Va.: Alban Institute, 1997.

Gaillardetz, Richard R. *Ecclesiology for a Global Church: A People Called and Sent*. Maryknoll, N.Y.: Orbis, 2008.

Heim, S. Mark. *Salvations: Truth and Difference in Religion*. Maryknoll, N.Y.: Orbis, 1995.

Jenkins, Philip. *The Next Christendom: The Coming of Global Christianity*. Rev. and updated ed. New York: Oxford University Press, 2007.

Lingenfelter, Sherwood G., and Marvin K. Mayers. *Ministering Cross-Culturally: An Incarnational Model for Personal Relationships*. Grand Rapids: Baker Academic, 2003.

Nessan, Craig L. *Orthopraxis or Heresy: The North American Theological Response to Latin American Liberation Theology*. Atlanta: Scholars, 1989.

Sanneh, Lamin. *Disciples of All Nations: Pillars of World Christianity*. New York: Oxford University Press, 2007.

Stackhouse, Max L., Tim Dearborn, and Scott R. Paeth, eds. *The Local Church in a Global Era: Reflections for a New Century*. Eugene, Ore.: Wipf & Stock, 2005.

Walls, Andrew F. *Mission in the Twenty-First Century: Exploring the Five Marks of Global Mission*. Edited by Cathy Ross. Maryknoll, N.Y.: Orbis, 2008.

FOR REFLECTION AND DISCUSSION

1. What does the word *catholic* mean to you? How can your congregation help reclaim the fullness of this description of the church?

2. Why does the Christian gospel have centrifugal force? What impresses you about the story of Christian mission to the ends of the earth?

3. What is at stake in the tension between Christianity and nationalism? How can one be patriotic and still give ultimate loyalty to God?

4. How have you experienced connections with the global church? What influence have these relationships had on your understanding of the nature of the Christian church?

5. What has your congregation done to accent global connections? What new initiatives might be taken to develop global awareness and partnerships?

Chapter Eleven

Ecumenism: That All May Be One

The great watchword for the ecumenical movement in the twentieth century was uttered by Jesus as a central petition of his high-priestly prayer in John 17:20-21: "I ask not only on behalf of these, but also on behalf of those who will believe in me through their word, that they may all be one. As you, Father, are in me and I am in you, may they also be in us, so that the world may believe that you have sent me." Notice that the prayer for the unity of the church is not formulated as an end in itself. Rather, Jesus prays about the unity of the church *for the sake of mission*. The unity of the persons in the Holy Trinity serves as an analogy for understanding the unity of the church with God. The church's unity in God serves as powerful testimony for the sake of the world, "that the world may believe" in Jesus as the one God has sent.

Christ entrusted to the church the Sacraments of baptism and the Eucharist as signs of its oneness with him. All who have been baptized in the name of Christ have been baptized into one body and made to drink of one Spirit (1 Cor 12:13). Likewise, Paul queries the congregation in Corinth: "The cup of blessing that we bless, is it not a sharing in the blood of Christ? The bread that we break, is it not a sharing in the body of Christ? Because there is one bread, we who are many are one body, for we all partake of the one bread" (1 Cor 10:16-17).

However, one does not need to know much about the Christian church (even the congregation at Corinth) to learn that these very Sacraments of unity have become the source of bitter arguments and deep division throughout its history. The splintering of the church into thousands of denominations, sects, and factions functions as one of the greatest obstacles to belief on the part of the world. The church's fragmentation makes a mockery of Jesus' prayer and of the Sacraments of unity which he instituted.

If the world is to believe that Jesus is indeed the one sent by God, ecumenical rapprochement remains an urgent priority. Even more, the responsibility for ecumenical reconciliation needs to shift from official dialogues and inter-confessional agreements to the local level, where the implications of reconciliation can have immediate and concrete ramifications. How can we continue to confess our faith in the words of the Nicene Creed—"We believe in the *one* . . . church"—and continue to exist alienated and even antagonistic to other members of the one body of Christ?

Ecumenism as Apologetics

"Why should I believe all this stuff when you Christians can't even get along with each other?" In these or similar words, the divisions within the church give offense (and excuse!) to nonbelievers. Whether we consider Protestants and Roman Catholics in Northern Ireland, estranged Lutheran church bodies in the United States, or proselytizing by the "non-denominational" church down the street, the fragmentation of the church is a scandal to skeptics—as it ought to be to Christians themselves.

One should not confuse this proposal about the unity of the church as an attempt to impose uniformity. Already prior to the formation of the New Testament canon, the church had attained a rich diversity of communal expressions, reflected in the variety of theological images used to interpret God's reality as revealed in the person and work of Jesus. Moreover, local communities of faith accented different aspects of the Christian tradition according to the particular circumstances and the diverse problems confronting them. Thus each of the four Gospel writers—Matthew, Mark, Luke, and John—formulated their version of the Jesus story in correlation with the issues facing the particular community to which they related. In a parallel way, Paul wrote letters employing varying theological images and different practical instructions depending on the situation of the congregation he was addressing.

There is strong evidence that the major confessional differences between the various churches can be explained on the basis of the New Testament itself. The variety of outlooks and theological positions within the canon itself accounts for a large portion of the significant divergences of belief among the denominations. Thus, Lutherans give central place to the Pauline doctrine of justification by grace through faith; Presbyterians emphasize the glory of God in worship and life; Methodists focus on living a sanctified life; and Pentecostals stress the extraordinary gifts of the Holy Spirit. Each of these emphases (as well as others) has a legitimate place among the varied writings in the New Testament canon. Different "canons within the canon" lead various church bodies in distinct theological directions. Extrapolating the logical conclusions, these contrasting points of orientation serve to explain most of the key confessional differences among the Christian denominations.

A reconciled church would need to make provision for a comparable range of theological interpretations, varieties of piety, and differences of church order as are evidenced in the New Testament itself. Yet within such a reconciled church, one could also hope for the mutual affirmation of the legitimacy of one another's ministries which is sorely lacking between so many churches in the present. The greatest affront of all is the failure on the part of churches to recognize one another's baptism. To rebaptize someone from another tradition is tantamount to denying that other tradition is Christian.

A similar argument can be made with regard to the failure of Christians to welcome one another at their celebrations of the Lord's Supper. One might do well to ask whether a celebration of the Lord's Supper at which some of the baptized (that is, those from another denomination) are not welcome is a legitimate celebration at all. The Jesus who ate at table with tax collectors and sinners scandalized only the Pharisees. The Jesus who shared a meal with his disciples the night before his death was crucified for all. Jesus' supper is to be a meal for the forgiveness of sins and the reconciliation of the estranged. How tragic that we have invented reasons for turning it into an occasion for excluding members of Christ's body who happen to belong to another denomination!

Although the first great schism of the church occurred in 1054, with the split between the Orthodox and Roman Catholic churches, it is the fallout from the Protestant Reformation that has led to the bewildering array of sects and brands of churches with which we are today confronted. While the recovery of the central doctrine of justification by grace through faith was an absolutely necessary correction insisted upon by the reformers of the late Medieval church, the consequences for the unity of the church have been disastrous. By introducing the principle of conscience as a central basis for determining the legitimacy of the interpretation of Scripture, the floodgates were opened to a torrent of waters wreaking destruction upon the church's oneness. Each and every religious visionary too easily claims a special revelation of divine truth and proclaims it with such intensity that some are persuaded to follow.

The churches of the Reformation, and particularly the Lutherans among them, bear a special measure of responsibility for the fragmenting of the church in subsequent centuries. This in no way negates the historical necessity of the reforms demanded by Luther and the reformers of the Roman Catholic Church in the sixteenth century. It is, however, to honestly confess the Protestant share of responsibility for the loss of church unity, which was an unforeseeable yet tragic consequence of the Reformation heritage. For this reason, Protestants—and particularly Lutherans—have a special obligation to commit themselves to the reconciliation of Christ's church. By God's grace, Lutherans may also be uniquely situated to serve as a bridge in the process of reconciliation between those churches with the "historic episcopate" and other Reformed churches who share Lutheran commitment to the authority of Scripture alone.

For the sake of the gospel and Christian mission in the twenty-first century (a century where we continue to see further erosion of Christian influence), ecumenism emerges as an apologetic task of the first order.

What is more, only a reconciled Christian church, in which the mission of Jesus Christ is placed ahead of denominational wrangling, will be adequately prepared for the societal and environmental problems of this new century.

Toward a Common Table

As one surveys the alienation among church bodies during the first four hundred years following the Reformation, the progress toward reuniting divided Christendom accomplished in the last decades is remarkable. When at Amsterdam in 1948 two strands of the ecumenical movement, "Faith and Order" and "Life and Work," united in the formation of the World Council of Churches (WCC), this marked the culmination of a process that had been fermenting for decades, even prior to the war. Following a pattern of holding global assemblies approximately every seven years, the WCC defined itself with these words at New Delhi in 1961: "The World Council of Churches is a fellowship of churches which confess the Lord Jesus Christ as God the Savior according to the Scriptures and therefore seek to fulfill together their common calling to the glory of the one God, Father, Son and Holy Spirit."

The scope of the WCC expanded greatly beginning in 1960, when Pope John XXIII authorized the participation of the Roman Catholic Church in the ecumenical movement by forming the Society for Promoting Christian Unity. Further impetus was given to Roman Catholic involvement by the Decree on Ecumenism, adopted at the Second Vatican Council in 1964. Now the deliberations of the WCC could include not only Protestant and Orthodox viewpoints but also Roman Catholic representation.

One of the fruits of the ecumenical movement has been the promotion and organization of bilateral and multilateral dialogues among church bodies. The purpose of such conversations has been to search for the convictions which churches share in common, while not minimizing those issues that continue to divide. The results of these dialogues have been published in numerous volumes, many of which have been given official status by church bodies.

Perhaps the most important product of all these ecumenical discussions has been the consensus proposal, *Baptism, Eucharist and Ministry*, disseminated to the churches by the Commission on Faith and Order of the WCC meeting at Lima in 1982. This document called upon all churches to respond to its formulation of a proposed consensus position regarding the key issues of baptism, Eucharist, and ministry. The question posed was a crucial one: "To what extent can your church recognize in this text the faith of the Church through the ages?" It is exactly this sort of exacting question that can move the denominations to self-examination regarding the fullness of their own positions and acknowledge the legitimacy of Christian truth in other bodies. This proposal evoked a voluminous literature of differentiated responses.

Efforts of the WCC like this one, together with the many bilateral and multilateral dialogues, have borne exceptional fruit in increasing mutual understanding and cooperation among the divided churches. Specific proposals continue to come before denominational assemblies seeking ratification. Consequently, several church bodies have entered into "full communion" agreements with one another, allowing for table fellowship and, in some cases, the orderly exchange of ordained ministers.

The central problem with this process has been, however, the failure of the reception process to shift from the denominational to the local level. The true test for the success of the ecumenical movement is now located on the level of relationships among local congregations in local communities throughout the world. Insofar as the groundwork for ecumenical rapprochement has not been carefully developed on the local level, the adoption of new and innovative proposals—especially those that could have substantive impact on local communities—remains difficult.

The future of the ecumenical movement shifts increasingly to local congregations, who must assume responsibility for deliberating what unity means among the churches in a particular place. Guided by the careful statements of theologians and church executives, congregations need to encourage substantive conversation in their local communities to discover the implications of ecumenical dialogue for their own congregational life and mission. Already this has begun to take place to a certain degree in some locales. But the initiatives have often been cursory rather than involving our best efforts at dialogue and study. Where significant discussion has evolved, the implications for common worship and outreach are many.

One perennial danger of the congregation is parochialism. We become so preoccupied with our own inner life as a congregation that it is difficult to generate the energy needed to initiate programs between congregations, particularly with those of another denomination. Perhaps the only cure for such lethargy is to immerse ourselves ever more deeply in Jesus' high-priestly prayer, so that our hearts may be converted to the urgency of the ecumenical task for the sake of Christian mission.

A glance in any local phone directory will shock the reader at the wide array of churches listed in the yellow pages. In most communities, an interdenominational ministerium likely meets. These provide one forum for ecumenical discussion, although the wide range of viewpoints at such gatherings may make substantive discussion laborious. Such organizations are often much more adept at cooperating on practical expressions of Christian charity than entering into serious theological discussion. If we probe too deeply, we might soon discover how much our interpretations of the faith separate us! This is not to dismiss efforts to promote theologically motivated ecumenical discussion among ministerial alliances. It is only to acknowledge the difficulty of the enterprise.

A more manageable approach to local ecumenical efforts begins with cooperation among a limited number of congregations, perhaps starting with two. Insofar as these come from traditions that have engaged in dialogue on the denominational level, the published resources from such dialogues are invaluable for deepening the conversation. Those who give leadership to whatever meetings are planned between the churches must give careful attention to such materials. One aim of local ecumenical conversation is to measure the degree to which the issues that surface in formal denominational discussion also truly inform the differences that exist in local practice. Sometimes one discovers that on the local level what unites and what divides are based on factors quite different from what we might assume based on confessional traditions.

One valuable gift from local ecumenical conversations is the human relationships that develop out of such encounters. Something that inhibits enthusiasm for ecumenical events among congregations is the fear by some members of not knowing enough and thereby demonstrating ignorance about one's own tradition (or perhaps disclosing the vices of one's congregation) in the presence of another. The contrary, however, is virtually always the case. We discover in conversation with others how much we already implicitly know about our own traditions and, moreover, how committed we are to the congregation to which we belong. The relationships we establish with Christians from a congregation in another tradition only enhance our own experience of community in Christ.

Relationships between congregations must be nurtured over a long period of time. While not wanting to spread one's efforts too thin, a congregation may be able to pursue more than one ecumenical relationship at a time, working separately with congregations that come from distinct traditions. Careful attention needs to be paid to the agendas for the time spent together. The meetings must not be allowed to function merely as social gatherings but rather give focus to issues that might lead to deeper understanding of one another's traditions and to mutual ventures in intercongregational cooperation.

One central goal of ecumenical relationships between local congregations is the planning and holding of joint worship services. These should be scheduled at a time that encourages maximum participation from congregation members. That means considering Sunday morning as a prime time to hold common worship. What better witness to the community at large about the unity of Christ's church than to organize and publicize shared worship on a Sunday morning!

Certainly there are other times in the year that also offer advantages. The festivals of Epiphany and Ascension are often underobserved by congregations, and excitement for worship on these days can be stimulated by planning a joint service. Reformation Day (or Sunday) can offer an occasion for congregations from different Reformation traditions to celebrate their heritage. All Saints Day provides an occasion for churches from every denomination to emphasize their unity and may be a particularly good time for Roman Catholics to join with Protestants at worship.

Pentecost affords the opportunity to accent the gifts poured upon the church by the Holy Spirit, including the gift of unity.

Congregations that do not observe the liturgical year have their own patterns, which may give reason to an ecumenical observance at a given time of year. Good Friday has become an occasion for community-wide services. Of course, national holidays, such as Thanksgiving, may give impetus to ecumenical services that otherwise would not take place.

Prior to such ecumenical worship, careful planning must take place to ensure that those involved will understand and appreciate the ritual action. For example, what one tradition assumes to belong to the standard repertoire of hymns may prove to be totally unfamiliar to those from another ecclesial tradition. Unspoken assumptions can be extremely dangerous. The congregation hosting an ecumenical service should probably take the lead in ordering the worship held in its own worship space, using a liturgy from its own tradition. At the same time, every effort should be spent to inform members of the other congregation(s) about the ritual practices and their meaning. Members of the guest congregation(s) can be invited to lead portions of the service where appropriate. The clergy of both congregations can share the leadership in a way that demonstrates mutual affirmation of one another's ministries. On another occasion, the roles between host and guest congregations can be reversed.

The ultimate expression of congregational unity in Christ occurs around the Lord's Table. Where denominations have reached agreements regarding full communion or interim Eucharistic sharing, a common celebration of the Eucharist provides the culminating symbol of Christian unity. Thankfully, a number of Christian traditions have reached the point where their Communion tables are officially open to members of certain other denominations. Again, such mutual celebrations of the Lord's Supper must be carefully planned by the participating churches, lest differences in practice undermine the unity contained in the symbols of one loaf and one cup.

Where denominational differences do not yet permit eucharistic sharing (or even common worship), may our hunger for sharing this universal Christian meal motivate us to renewed efforts at reconciliation!

What a tragedy if the first time we join together at table will be in God's heaven!

In Service to God's World

Concerted efforts at community service are a powerful form of Christian witness by congregations of different denominations. We recall Jesus' prayer for the church to be one, in order that the world might believe that Jesus is the one sent from God. Common acts of Christian charity by congregations in a local community thereby have a twofold purpose. First, they aim to be responsive to pressing human needs in that community. Those who are hungry, homeless, lacking clothing, suffering discrimination, addicted, or abused need both the material help and advocacy efforts that Christian churches can provide. Second, however, our ministry to human need is itself a form of witness to the power of Jesus Christ alive in that place.

Churches should neither use their evangelistic motive to manipulate those to whom they minister nor remain silent about the name of the one they seek to serve. To balance genuine concern for those in physical need with a holistic concern also for the soul requires tremendous integrity of purpose. Cooperative efforts on the part of churches are often threatened by disagreements about how acts of mercy should serve the cause of evangelism. On the one side are those who make material help conditional upon listening to an evangelistic message. On the other side are those who avoid naming the name of Jesus altogether. Finding a middle ground between these extremes, cooperative efforts at Christian charity do and ought to make clear witness to Jesus Christ as the one sent by God. Clarity from the outset about how charity and evangelism are to be related will help avoid tension in ecumenical ventures at social outreach.

The specific needs of the community should set the priorities for which projects a local ecumenical organization ought to undertake. In virtually every community, there is a pressing need to respond to the hungry, the homeless, those suffering discrimination, the abused, the addicted, and the transient. Given the cutbacks in government services, the urgency of a response by Christians continues to increase. The weight of human need may appear by far to surpass the resources of the church to respond. For this reason it is wise for leaders of ecumenical efforts to analyze carefully which needs deserve the highest priority and which needs the group is best equipped to meet given the limited resources available.

One value of cooperative effort in responding to the hungry, homeless, or transient is the ability to ensure good stewardship of resources. A coordinated effort helps avoid duplication of services among individual congregations. Common record keeping can assist in tracking the assistance given to various persons and families in order to balance the distribution of limited resources. Those eligible for government services can be more easily identified and referred. Not least of all, those who contribute their resources to the support of local charity gain confidence that more effective use is being made of their gifts.

Local ecumenical efforts need not always start from scratch in developing programs of social outreach. Church World Service can assist in coordinating local efforts on behalf of the hungry through its CROP Walk program. This program, which can become an annual event, both raises awareness of the needs of the hungry and provides an effective way of raising funds. Habitat for Humanity is another nationwide organization that can give direction to local efforts, in this case providing housing to the homeless. Apart from such large-scale organizations, the models of social ministry developed in other nearby communities can give direction to local initiatives.

Community-wide efforts to develop food pantries, homeless shelters, safe houses for abused women and children, treatment centers for the addicted, or assistance for transients are not the only possible results of ecumenical cooperation among local congregations. Where as few as two congregations are willing to work together, perhaps as a result of a carefully cultivated partnership, valuable fruits can become manifest. Among those projects that can be undertaken by as few as two congregations are a shared program of Christian education (for example, Vacation Bible School), the formation of a preschool, cooperation in making quilts for use in local shelters or overseas, outreach among youth, or a soup kitchen for the hungry.

Given the incredible cost of building and maintaining a facility, one of the wisest stewardship decisions that two congregations might make would be sharing the use of a single building. Such a decision requires a congregation be clear that its identity is not grounded in its exclusive use of a particular building (the "edifice complex"). Instead, it challenges a congregation to think anew that the church is not a building but rather the members themselves are the body of Christ, with Jesus Christ as the head. Where two congregations come to the point where they so fully affirm one another's ministries that the sharing of a building is possible, again a powerful witness is made to a local community.

Another dimension of ecumenical witness involves public advocacy on behalf of the marginalized and oppressed in a given community. When dealing with the most controversial issues and advocating social change, it will prove difficult for a ministerial alliance to come to a consensus on a given course of action. Instead, certain members of congregations may well come together to work for advocacy according to their particular vision of a better future. Further comment on the place of ecumenical efforts in advocating public policy will be reserved for the next chapter.

The theology of the congregation articulated in this chapter elevates the role of ecumenism to a status seldom attained by congregations in the present. Ecumenism gives expression to one of the key dimensions of a congregation's mission. In part, this is due to the exigencies of mission in this post-Christian era. But even more fundamentally, it is in response to the prayer of Jesus that the church should be one. The scandal of a divided Christendom does not serve the mission of the one Lord, Jesus Christ. We are called to reclaim the oneness of baptism as we gather around a common Lord's Table, in order to witness to Jesus Christ as the one sent by God for the salvation of the entire world. United in this mission we stand; divided we fall.

FOR FURTHER READING

Bos, A. David. *Bound Together: A Theology for Ecumenical Community Ministry.* Cleveland: Pilgrim, 2005.

Braaten, Carl E., and Robert W. Jenson, eds. *The Ecumenical Future.* Grand Rapids: Eerdmans, 2004.

Gros, Jeffrey, Eamon McManus, and Ann Riggs. *Introduction to Ecumenism.* Mahwah, N.J.: Paulist, 1997.

Hunsinger, George. *The Eucharist and Ecumenism: Let Us Keep the Feast.* Cambridge: Cambridge University Press, 2008.

Kinnamon, Michael, and Brian E. Cope, eds. *The Ecumenical Movement: An Anthology of Key Texts and Voices.* Grand Rapids: Eerdmans, 1997.

Lazareth, William H., ed. *Baptism, Eucharist and Ministry.* Faith and Order Paper No. 111. Geneva: WCC Publications, 1982.

Lehmann, Karl, and Wolfhart Pannenberg. *The Condemnations of the Reformation Era: Do They Still Divide?* Minneapolis: Fortress Press, 1990.

Lindbeck, George A., ed. *Justification and the Future of the Ecumenical Movement: The Joint Declaration on the Doctrine of Justification.* Collegeville, Minn.: Liturgical, 2003.

Lossky, Nicolas, et al., eds. *Dictionary of the Ecumenical Movement.* Grand Rapids: Eerdmans/World Council of Churches, 2003.

Murphy, Francesca Aran, and Christopher Asprey, eds. *Ecumenism Today: The Universal Church in the Twenty-First Century.* Burlington: Ashgate, 2008.

Rusch, William G. *Ecumenical Reception: Its Challenge and Opportunity.* Grand Rapids: Eerdmans, 2007.

Sagovsky, Nicolas. *Ecumenism, Christian Origins, and the Practice of Communion.* Cambridge: Cambridge University Press, 2008.

FOR REFLECTION AND DISCUSSION

1. Why does Jesus pray for the unity of his followers? How have you experienced the blessings of church unity? How have you been offended by church divisions?

2. Give examples of how the differences between denominations are grounded in the diversity of perspectives in the New Testament. How does such an understanding of differences allow for "reconciled diversity"?

3. How has your church body been involved in ecumenical dialogue? You may want to refer to the publications or webpage of your denomination to explore this question.

4. What have been some of the best experiences of your congregation in ecumenical cooperation? What have been some of the challenges to ecumenical cooperation in your community?
5. What new initiatives in ecumenical dialogue and partnership can you imagine for your congregation? How might you get started?

Chapter Twelve

Social Ministry:
Striving for Justice
and Peace in All the Earth

D<small>o</small> you intend to continue in the covenant God made with you in Holy Baptism: to live among God's faithful people . . . and to strive for justice and peace in all the earth?"

This is the promise made according to the rite of Affirmation of Baptism, used at services of baptismal renewal by all the baptized, for the reception of new members, and especially for confirmation. To make such a promise is a tall order for one mature in the Christian faith, let alone a fourteen-year-old on confirmation day. This question aims to promote nothing less than the public responsibility of Christians in the world.

To enter the sphere of advocating public policy is to tread among serpents. The conviction remains strong among the baptized that a strict distinction must be maintained between church and state. This provision, intended to prevent the establishment of a state religion in the United States, is understood by many to preclude the church from taking stands on social issues. Suggesting that the church as a whole, or even that an individual congregation, take a position with regard to a controversial public issue is to invite snakebite.

Leaders of congregations who seek to fulfill the charge to strive for justice and peace in all the earth enter an arena that is highly contested and politically polarized. While the ministry of a congregation is impoverished by the failure to enter the fray, those who give leadership in such matters are called upon to follow the injunction of Jesus to "be wise as serpents and innocent as doves" (Matt 10:16).

Jesus leaves no room for the weak-hearted, however, when it comes to the task of social ministry. In one of the most frequently cited texts of liberation theology, we are summoned before the very judgment seat of Christ (Matt 25:31-45). Christ sits upon the throne of glory and separates the sheep from the goats, the saved from the damned. On what basis does Christ render judgment? On the basis of whether the members of the church rendered him merciful service in this world! And how did they render Christ service? On the basis of whether the hungry neighbor was fed, the thirst of the neighbor was quenched, the stranger was welcomed, the naked were clothed, the sick received ministry, and the prisoner was visited. For, you see, "as you did it to one of the least of these who are members of my family, you did it to me" (Matt 25:40). While the sheep in the parable were surprised to discover that Christ appeared in the form of the "least of these," we have an advantage they did not have and are therefore without excuse. We even have the witness of the one who was raised from the dead (cf. Luke 16:31), who instructs us according to the imperative of neighbor love.

Social Service and Social Advocacy

When reflecting on congregational social ministry, a fundamental distinction needs to be made between two unique expressions: social service and social advocacy. By "social service" we refer to those forms of social ministry that provide direct assistance to relieve human need. One might think immediately of disaster relief, hunger programs, medical assistance, or housing projects. Also falling into this category are many of the common forms of denominational social service agencies: adoption programs, counseling services, refugee resettlement, job training, homeless shelters, sheltered workshops for those with disabilities, assistance to people who are blind or deaf, support for single parents, programs for the elderly, and a host of other charitable works.

Congregations participate in an essential way in social service through their financial support and by volunteer efforts given to denominational, regional, and ecumenical programs organized to offer direct relief to various kinds of human suffering and need. A local congregation might also have such ministries as a food pantry, day care center, parochial school or preschool, short-term housing shelter, refugee sponsorship, safe house, or providing funds for those in acute need (for example, travelers' aid, utilities assistance, rent assistance, and so forth). This is to leave unmentioned the ministry provided by members of a congregation for each other, lending emotional, material, and spiritual support in times of crisis (in times of illness, death, accident, disaster, job loss, marital crisis, depression, and so on). A "ministry of presence" to those who suffer acute human need can itself be a vital form of congregational social ministry.

All of these forms of "social service" are essential, necessary, and exemplary demonstrations of social ministry. Congregational support for such programs on a local, regional, or global level provides a powerful witness about Christian compassion to those in need. Through these efforts great human suffering finds relief. Such activities, moreover, provide an outlet for Christian charity that builds upon strong precedents in the history of the church, beginning in the New Testament. A clear consensus in favor of these kinds of programs emerges naturally within the life of a congregation.

When we turn to social advocacy, however, we enter an arena that is highly contested. By "social advocacy" we mean efforts on the part of the church to change societal structures, promote economic policies, or enact legislation that is consistent with its understanding of the kingdom of God. The charters of organizations like Bread for the World and Amnesty International provide a reference point for this distinctive type of social ministry. Denominational advocacy efforts with regard to racism, sexism, heterosexism, poverty, hunger, homelessness, violence, war, arms proliferation, prisons, capital punishment, environmental concern, and so forth fall into this category. Likewise congregations, or members thereof, may wish to raise their voices on behalf of a particular cause that entails changing societal structures.

Unlike proposals involving social service, however, congregations often have a difficult time arriving at a consensus around questions of social advocacy. The provision for the separation of church and state in the U.S. Constitution is often interpreted to deny church advocacy with regard to political, economic, and social causes. While this is a misinterpretation of the disestablishment clause (its purpose being to forbid the state from establishing a favored religion), confusion about or resistance to congregational advocacy efforts is common among many church members.

This misunderstanding of the church's efforts in social advocacy requires a critical reappraisal. The biblical tradition bears witness to an extraordinary "justice trajectory" that warrants the church's involvement in advocacy on behalf of the poor, victims of violence, the marginalized, and the oppressed. Beginning with the exodus narrative, God hears and responds to the groaning of Hebrew slaves (Exod 2:23-25) and acts to set them free from Pharaoh's oppression (Exod 3:7-9). A distinguishing characteristic of the law by which Israel was to live out its covenant relationship with God is the provision by which there is to be special protection for the widow, orphan, and "resident alien" (Exod 22:21-24). The poor likewise receive protection from paying exploitative interest and from excessive demands for "security deposits" on loans (Exod 22:25-27). Two of the most remarkable aspects of the Leviticus legal code are the standards for a sabbatical year and a year of jubilee (Lev 25). Both of these provisions are based on the conviction that God ultimately owns everything. Accordingly, in the seventh year the land is to lie fallow and the economy is to be sustained only by what has been stored and by the fields' natural yield (Lev 25:1-7). More extraordinary still is the account of the "jubilee year," to be observed every fiftieth year, in which all debts were to be canceled and property returned to ancestral estates (Lev 25:8-24).

When Israel came to be organized around the rule of a king—a decision about which controversy prevailed for fear of the king's abuse of power—it was with the expectation that the king would himself serve God's law with its demand for justice (2 Sam 8:15; 1 Kgs 10:9). Several of the psalms articulate the expectation that the king advocate justice and righteousness, especially in defense of the poor and oppressed (Pss 58, 72, 82). At the very same time as Israel adopted the monarchy, there emerged simultaneously the office of prophet as a check on the potential abuses of royal power. The oracles of the prophets redound with the demand that Israel and its ruler do justice (for example, Mic 3:9-12; Jer 22:13-16; Isa 42:5-7). The Messiah for whom Israel longed would be the executor of justice and peace (Isa 11:1-9).

This strong justice trajectory within the Hebrew Bible finds its continuation in the ministry of Messiah Jesus. In Luke's Gospel, for example, Jesus is programmatically identified as the fulfillment of Isaiah's messianic expectations in his inaugural sermon at Nazareth (Luke 4:16-21). Jesus' teachings contain a powerful message of justice for the poor and judgment upon the rich (Luke 6:20-26; 12:15-21, 33-34; 16:13, 19-31; 18:22-25; 19:1-10). Jesus provokes his opponents by driving the sellers out of the temple, declaring: "My house shall be a house of prayer; but you have made it a den of robbers" (Luke 19:45-46). Jesus is renowned as the friend of tax collectors and sinners who are invited to eat with him at table (Luke 15:1-2). In accordance with covenantal law, Jesus advocates the cause of the poor, the sick, the marginalized, and the oppressed. Luke witnesses that in Jesus' ministry the messianic age has arrived.

While this justice trajectory is upheld in the Synoptic traditions and to a certain degree in the other traditions of the earliest church (Acts 2:42-47; 4:32-37), the New Testament expectation about an imminent Parousia raised a pointed challenge to the very idea of social transformation (1 Thess 4:13-18). The expectation of the near return of Jesus as the Son of Man to bring history to its conclusion undercut efforts at working for social change (1 Cor 7:17-24). Why invest in the structures of an age that is soon to pass away? Charity offered in relief of human suffering is always salutary. But to advocate the change of social structures within the context of Roman oppression, especially within a scenario of imminent apocalyptic destruction and deliverance, was unimaginable (Rev 22:12-21).

Contrary to the expectations of first-century Christians, we have witnessed the unfolding of two thousand years of Christian history. While some will continue to insist that the return of Christ is imminent (all the more with the drama of each new political crisis!), we cannot continue to allow the eschatological expectations of the first century to deter the church from investing in serious efforts at transforming the structures of this world on behalf of justice. This is not to argue for any utopian scheme by which Christians can themselves construct the kingdom of God. Rather, it is to argue that the church rightfully has a theological warrant to engage in social advocacy according to the justice trajectory inherited from Israel and sustained in the ministry of Jesus. While the most we could ever hope for in this world are approximations of God's justice, many lives are salvaged by reasoned and organized efforts to establish more just social structures.

In anticipation of the continuation of history, we take our bearings for social advocacy not from New Testament apocalyptic but from the Hebrew concept of *shalom*. The word *shalom* expresses the conviction that the divine purpose for this world is that all created beings live together in justice, righteousness, and peace. The salvation that God intends is not an escape from this world but rather its transformation. *Shalom* entails a holistic understanding of salvation in which body and spirit, the individual and society, the human and nonhuman, the religious and the political, are all incorporated. God seeks to work "total well-being" for the entire creation (Folk).

The Critical Mass: Three Priorities

Taking cues from the Eucharist liturgy and the contemporary context, we propose three priorities for congregational social ministry. The structure of the Eucharist—as we in worship enact the kingdom of God—provides a mirror in which we see the conditions of our world more clearly. The "mass" thus contains a "critical" element; it helps us see our world in the light of God's *shalom*. The three features of the liturgy to which we attend are: (1) the offering of the created gifts of bread and wine for the meal, (2) the sharing of the food around the table, and (3) the passing of the peace of Christ within the community and beyond.

First, the offering of elements from God's good creation for the meal symbolizes the responsibility of Christians to care for God's world. One offertory prayer reminds the worshiping community to be dedicated to the care of all God has made. In recent years, there have been poignant reminders that there are limits to the earth's ability to recover from abuse. Natural resources can be depleted. Plant and animal species do become extinct. Pollution does damage not only to the air we breathe but especially to the ozone layer. Global warming is causing irreversible and destructive climate change. Water can be made hazardous for creaturely consumption and habitation. Nuclear materials pose a long-term threat to life in all its manifestations. All of life inhabits a delicate ecosystem, existing in delicate symbiotic relationships. When one part of the ecosystem suffers, all members of the system suffer together (cf. 1 Cor 12).

Congregations have a responsibility before God to care for the portion of God's creation entrusted to their stewardship. This begins with care for the congregation's own property and grounds, but extends far beyond. Congregations can do much to educate about proper care for the earth, sky, and sea. Members can hear, for example, about recycling efforts and the responsible reduction and disposal of waste. They can take seriously the environmental impact of congregational decisions. They can take the perspective of a steward of God's creation into their homes and their places of employment.

More than local efforts, however, congregations can encourage members to become advocates for legislation consistent with sound stewardship of God's world. There are a number of groups that alert a broad membership about the environmental implications of public decisions. Proposals are offered for intelligent advocacy on behalf of the creation upon which we all depend for life. Congregations can themselves become vehicles for communicating issues of public policy to members.

Second, the sharing of bread and wine around the Communion table serves as a powerful reminder of the responsibility to feed hungry neighbors. We live in a hungry world. Jesus fed the multitudes (Mark 6:30-44; 8:1-10). Can we begin to assimilate what it means that thirty thousand hungry neighbors continue to die every day from hunger and its related causes? Over one billion human beings are seriously malnourished in our world. The scale of human hunger exceeds our capacity to fathom. Hunger is a scandal that has lost its ability to shock our consciences. All current statistics, moreover, indicate the disparity between the rich and poor, the "haves" and "have nots," continues to increase. Population numbers rise while the willingness of the privileged to share declines. Violence against the earth—pollution, soil erosion, desertification, resource depletion—together with the use of inappropriate technology reduces the amount of food that local agriculture can produce. Feedlot cattle eat grain while human beings starve. Will the amount of suffering related to hunger be so magnified in coming decades that the church will be compelled to declare ending hunger a matter of *status confessionis?*

Congregations are obligated to include ministry to hungry neighbors at the heart of their social ministry efforts. This begins with relief to hungry members of the congregation itself. One in ten households in the U.S. is living with hunger or risk of hunger, most of these children. Financial resources can be made available to assist in the feeding of needy individuals and families. Local food pantries provide a way to extend this concern into the larger community. Many congregations may also choose to participate in meal delivery programs (for example, Meals on Wheels). These and other forms of direct relief to hungry people belong to the identity and mission of those who seek to serve in the name of the one who fed the multitudes.

If the dimensions of the hunger dilemma are to be adequately addressed, however, members of congregations will need to become increasingly committed to engagement in ending hunger on a larger scale. Supporting denominational hunger programs at a significant level of financial commitment is fundamental. Such programs address systemic issues, which need to be taken seriously in the effective stewardship of resources. Denominational programs aim both at direct relief of hunger and at the development of local economies so that people become capacitated to feed themselves.

Furthermore, members of congregations need to become educated on the impact which legislation has on the hungry, both domestically and globally. Just as Jesus expressed particular concern for the poor in his ministry, so the church of Jesus has the responsibility to act as advocate for the poor who have lost the voice to speak for themselves. Citizens have become woefully inept at examining legislation according to any criterion other than self-interest. As Robert Bellah and others have argued, we desperately need to recover a notion of the common good. Members of congregations need to measure and evaluate all legislation according to its impact on the poor of this world. Moreover, advocacy to end hunger is a matter not only of Christian charity but of self-interest in order to build stable political and economic structures throughout the world.

Third, the passing of the peace within the Eucharist liturgy symbolizes the imperative that Christians act as peacemakers (Matt 5:9). Not only are we to be at peace with one another as we come to the table, but, as we encounter in the supper the one who is the Prince of Peace, we are filled with a peace that makes us advocates of peace.

Violence permeates every level of modern society. Domestic violence invades the home. The entertainment industry portrays countless acts of violence that make it appear commonplace. Neighborhoods are stalked by gang violence. Weapons proliferate in our homes, workplaces, and even schools. Violent crime seems rampant and random. Society retaliates against violent crime by executing capital punishment. Terrorist acts maim and kill the innocent. New forms of tribalism threaten to further disintegrate the social fabric, turning each faction against all others. War, buttressed by weapons of unimaginable destructive force, continues to break out season after season. Each new war is always declared a righteous cause, as the name of God is regularly invoked as rationale for each nation's involvement.

Of all peoples, Christians are those who ought to see through the rationalizations used to justify acts of violence. At the core of Christian conviction, we know the cross of Jesus Christ, which testifies to the violent death of an innocent man. Recent scholarship, under inspiration from the work of René Girard, has unmasked the proclivity of human beings to resolve tension and rivalry within society by acts of "sacred violence." As the ancient Jewish ritual of scapegoating was performed to transfer the guilt of the people to the ritual animal, so society repeatedly identifies victims who function as scapegoats to relieve societal stress. Whether or not one should argue that all religion originates with acts of sacred violence (as does Girard himself), it is imperative for us to critically examine how readily and with what motivation we turn to violence and scapegoating in order to resolve conflict.

If, as Girard argues, the cross of Jesus discloses the usually hidden power of the scapegoat mechanism, then Christians bear a responsibility to examine and criticize all acts of violence insofar as they mask the dynamics of scapegoating. One meaning of Jesus' death is that by this means "God was pleased to reconcile to himself all things, whether on earth or in heaven, by making peace through the blood of his cross" (Col 1:20). Christ died so we would stop scapegoating each other. Christ died that violence might cease and reconciliation prevail.

This means Christians claim as a core part of their mission the relief of suffering for victims of violence—whether in domestic situations, local communities, or international conflicts. But it means furthermore that Christians advocate legislation that establishes just relations as the basis for peace. As has been said before, those who seek peace must work for justice. Where conflict threatens, Christians must prophetically question premature attempts to resort to violence, scrutinizing the situation according to the scapegoat phenomenon and insisting on negotiation as the better course. It is in the public arena that Christians are challenged to realize the injunction: "Go in peace; serve the Lord."

The three priorities for social ministry cited in this chapter by no means exhaust the list of topics requiring faithful response by Christians. Other priorities also deserve serious attention: racism, sexism, and human rights, to name but a few others. Congregations need to be involved in addressing as many of these issues as possible. As a matter of fact, these additional issues intersect at many points with the subjects dealt with in this chapter. Care for God's creation, ending hunger, and making peace, however, are imperatives that belong on every congregation's social ministry agenda. The vision of God's *shalom* summons us to action.

Congregational Praxis

To provide congregational leadership for social ministry requires a carefully considered and wise strategy. Opinions will vary greatly whether congregations ought to get involved at all, let alone the question of which course of action should be followed. Those who give leadership in social ministry, particularly in advocacy efforts, must have a strong relationship of trust established with those members who will disagree. If the congregation is to serve as a community of moral deliberation, all members must commit themselves to mutual concern for one another as a foundation that is more secure than any disagreement about controversial issues. This is not to argue that controversy should be avoided. Indeed, some of the best courses of action are only discovered through the give and take of conflicting opinions. Such ought to be a matter of course in a democracy. But it remains the responsibility of leaders to measure the urgency of the social issue in relation to the ability of the congregation to sustain discord.

Leaders of congregations have the responsibility of listening carefully to members who have reservations regarding social advocacy in general as well as the objections they might have against a particular position. On the basis of such careful listening, leaders must next discern the "cutting edge" of the congregation in proposing a particular kind of involvement in social ministry. To operate at the cutting edge means to encourage social ministry responses that challenge members to ever deeper levels of engagement without provoking exaggerated reactions against such involvement. A leader must take pains in the process of discernment to ascertain just where the "cutting edge" might be. One seeks to lead exactly at that edge, neither lagging behind the consensus of the congregation nor leading too far out in front of the pack.

Leadership in social ministry involves examining the budget of a congregation and its commitment to benevolence. One of the key indicators of a congregation's mission consciousness is the percentage of the budget given toward the common ministry of the denomination and other benevolent causes. A congregation that is ready to direct a significant portion of its offerings toward local, regional, and global social ministry demonstrates that it understands how the congregation does not exist to be served but to serve the cause of the Christ who gave his life for the sake of others. Congregations need to remain ever vigilant in examining their budgetary priorities.

In selecting which social ministry projects to undertake, several factors deserve consideration. First, one must measure the gifts, abilities, and energy level of congregation members. One must make sure that the congregation has the capacity to complete the projects to which it commits. Second, one must analyze community and global needs to discover which problems deserve primary attention. Such needs must be prioritized because the number of possible involvements is infinite. Those needs initially identified on the basis of first impressions may prove on closer examination not to be the most appropriate outlet for a congregation's involvement. Third, one must devise an approach that does not rob the "recipients" of their dignity or their ability to act for themselves. Fourth, one should devise projects that have a manageable scope, so that there is clear focus on what can and cannot be reasonably accomplished. Fifth, longterm projects must include a strategy for continually involving new people in carrying out the work.

A congregational consensus will almost always be easier to attain in matters dealing with social service rather than those involving social advocacy. Congregations can build upon an established consensus regarding social service in developing a deeper understanding of the issues that require social advocacy. As one learns more about those who suffer as victims in need of Christian charity, one eventually is confronted with the question of how to more effectively change the circumstances under which people become victims in the first place. The link between social service and social advocacy is inexorable yet necessitates conscientious efforts at education in order to become transparent.

Where a congregational leader seeks a greater degree of engagement in social ministry than a particular congregation seems able to provide, or where one becomes frustrated by a congregation's inability to move into deeper involvement in social advocacy, energy can be channeled into ecumenical or secular organizations where a common cause can be shared with others who share a similar vision. Organizations like Bread for the World, Amnesty International, Sierra Club, or the Fellowship of Reconciliation offer opportunities for involvement in creative social transformation. These organizations often assist members in locating those who share their concern within a particular geographical area. As one becomes active in such a group, it is wise for pastors to have conversations with members of the congregation about making a distinction between one's personal involvement as a citizen and one's role as a representative of the congregation.

As we conclude our discussion of congregational social ministry, it is important to reiterate that social ministry is one of nine components in the model developed in this book. Its importance should neither be over-emphasized nor underemphasized as a vital dimension of congregational life. One particular danger with regard to social ministry is that its proper place becomes distorted. While the entire ministry of a congregation is impoverished where social service and social advocacy are insufficiently developed, the entire ministry of a congregation should not be reduced to social ministry. To discern and maintain proper balance in congregational social ministry is a perpetual task. But the stakes are too high not to undertake the challenges.

FOR FURTHER READING

Barndt, Joseph. *Understanding and Dismantling Racism: The Twenty-First Century Challenge to White America*. Minneapolis: Fortress Press, 2007.

Birch, Bruce C., and Larry L. Rasmussen. *Bible and Ethics in Christian Life*. Minneapolis: Augsburg Books, 1989.

Folk, Jerry. *Doing Theology, Doing Justice*. Minneapolis: Fortress Press, 1991.

Maguire, Daniel C. *A Moral Creed for All Christians*. Minneapolis: Fortress Press, 2005.

McCurley, Foster R., ed. *Social Ministry in the Lutheran Tradition*. Minneapolis: Fortress Press, 2008.

McGovern, George, Bob Dole, and Donald E. Messer. *Ending Hunger Now*. Minneapolis: Fortress Press, 2005.

Nessan, Craig L. *Give Us This Day: A Lutheran Proposal for Ending World Hunger*. Minneapolis: Augsburg Fortress, 2003.

————. *Many Members Yet One Body: Committed Same-Gender Relationships and the Mission of the Church*. Minneapolis: Augsburg Fortress, 2004.

Rasmussen, Larry L. *Earth Community, Earth Ethics.* Maryknoll, N.Y.: Orbis, 1998.

Sider, Ronald J. *Rich Christians in an Age of Hunger: Moving from Affluence to Generosity.* Nashville: Thomas Nelson, 2005.

Stark, Rodney. *The Rise of Christianity: How the Obscure, Marginal, Jesus Movement Became the Dominant Religious Force in the Western World in a Few Centuries.* San Francisco: HarperSanFrancisco, 1997.

Welch, Sharon D. *Real Peace, Real Security: The Challenges of Global Citizenship.* Minneapolis: Fortress Press, 2008.

FOR REFLECTION AND DISCUSSION

1. How did Jesus engage in social ministry? Why was Jesus concerned about the well-being of both bodies and souls?

2. What is the difference between social service and social advocacy? Why is it difficult for Christians to understand and claim the importance of social advocacy?

3. How has your congregation engaged in social service? Social advocacy? Evaluate the congregation's past involvements.

4. What do you see as the priorities for social ministry in your congregation? Where do the priorities of care for creation, ending hunger, and peacemaking fit in?

5. What agencies or organizations might be helpful to your congregation in developing its efforts in social ministry? Explore how you might get connected with these resources.

CONCLUSION: "ONE LONG EPICLESIS"

Congregations receive vigor from the Spirit of God, who in-spires them through worship. The "theology of the congregation" developed in this book gains its breath in the regular con-spiring of the baptized at Sunday worship. In each of the nine chapters dealing with various facets of congregational life, the connections with worship and liturgy have been made explicit. The reader is encouraged to employ creative imagination to continue this work of trans-spiring worship themes into congregational praxis.

The kingdom of God, which we imagine and God enacts at worship, must extend into the liturgy of daily life. God's Spirit intends more than ritual performance, as crucial as that might be for the sake of our conversion. The Spirit of God wills the transformation of our very lives and our world according to kingdom impulses. The movement from sanctuary to streets and back again thus defines the very rhythm of congregational existence.

The model of congregational life proposed in this book revolves around two foci: (1) the formation and preservation of Christian identity and (2) the movement of the congregation into the world in mission. In a sense, these two are reverse sides of a single coin. A church that knows its true identity does mission. A church engaged in mission enacts its fundamental identity.

Yet in institutional practice, the two, identity and mission, often become disjointed. Just as the relationships between faith and works, justification and justice, or the second and third articles of the creed tend to become severed, so congregations are tempted to dissect in practice what ought to be held together. It is for heuristic purposes that the two foci are here distinguished. If the model achieves its intended purpose, however, both will be maintained as indispensable and inseparable constituents of congregational life.

The theology of the congregation articulated here is designed to assist congregational leaders, lay and ordained, to examine theology and practice in their own contexts. The model is intended to function as a mirror by which to reflect upon the dynamics in one's own congregation. Please recall the critical leadership skill of listening, taking the time to pay attention to one's own context prior to advocating change. The various dimensions of congregational life examined in this model are likely already present in varied manifestations, though perhaps in attenuated forms.

Although each context summons forth unique permutations, the central foci of identity and mission deserve nurture in every congregation. Therefore, the worship life of the congregation, the components serving identity (prayer, education, life in community, and stewardship), and those serving mission (evangelizing, global connections, ecumenism, and social ministry) are envisioned as essential dimensions of every congregation's life. The scale at which larger congregations can address each of these components will naturally be different from the scale attainable among smaller ones. Nonetheless, each congregation can direct some attention to each of these nine components. To the degree to which any component is missing, one suspects a diminishment of congregational vitality.

In the Nicene Creed, we are reminded of the four classical marks of the church: one, holy, catholic, apostolic. These characteristics help us understand the fullness of the whole church in its breadth and scope. In a parallel way, the nine components of this theology of the congregation might be employed to measure the fullness of the life of a congregation. What does the one, holy, catholic, apostolic church look like on the local level? It attends to these nine matters: worship, prayer, education, life in community, stewardship, evangelizing, global connections, ecumenism, and social ministry.

The nine components of this model live in dynamic interrelationship one with another. While worship has been allotted prominence, all of the themes should be understood to inform each other mutually. For example, life in community understood as "friendship with the crucified" leads congregation members into organizing acts of social ministry on behalf of the least of Jesus' sisters and brothers. Developing global connections with distant members of Christ's church serves to further our education about the nature of Christ's body in the world. By no means should these nine components be understood as fixed and isolated categories. Creative congregational programs link them together in new and exciting combinations.

Congregational leaders are challenged to examine ministry in their local context according to the foci and components of this model. Over the course of a congregation's history, it will be important at certain junctures to emphasize one focus or component over others, to compensate for and balance potential distortions. A congregation that has suffered major conflict, on the one hand, may need to concentrate on rebuilding identity before intentionally focusing on mission themes. A lethargic congregation, on the other hand, may urgently need to recover its calling to engage in evangelizing or social ministry. Leaders must be wise in their discernment regarding which areas require chief attention at a given moment in a congregation's history. Articulating one's own theological vision for the congregation can assist greatly in analyzing present practice and inviting others into dialogue about future directions.

One potential caveat for this approach: it may leave the impression that congregational ministry is an end in itself. There is a serious danger of overvaluing what Christians do within and explicitly for their congregations. Conversely, leaders of congregations often appear to undervalue the service to the neighbor implicitly offered in the course of everyday life. Those who spend a lot of time at church meetings are considered "better" members than those who are "too busy" with their jobs. It would be a mistake to think about the ministry of the Christian congregation and its members according to such logic.

While this book aims to encourage faithful thinking about the theology undergirding congregational life, the ultimate reason for this or any other way of organizing congregations is sacrificial service to God and neighbor. By virtue of baptism, God in Christ has made a claim on the totality of our lives. Christians must comprehend that the service which they render in daily life, what is done in many and varied daily vocations (at home, school, and work), is no less service of God than that which takes place within the confines of a church building. The false dichotomy between what one does as a member of a congregation and what one does as a baptized child of God in the world must be overcome. Only then will we begin to realize the expansive vision of Luther's "priesthood of all believers."

We live, like generations before us, at a time when congregations are tested and tempted from every side. Some would argue that in this post-Christian age, it is doubtful whether the congregation can survive as a viable institution. Indeed, increasing financial pressures do threaten the survival of many congregations, forcing them to reconfigure or perish. A prevailing apocalyptic mood threatens to turn congregations inward upon themselves. Quick fixes that promise "church growth" promise to deliver instant results, but may really sell out the gospel in the process of attempting artificial re-spiration.

Clearly, congregations, as expressions of the church, can become perfunctory, routinized, hollow shells. In every time and place, the Christian congregation continually requires what Yves Congar calls "one long epiclesis," that is, the repeated invocation of the living Spirit of the living God to breathe life into its forms.

One crucial task of leaders is to invoke prayerfully the spirit of Christ to enliven all we intend to be and do as congregations. Without the invocation of the living Spirit of God, every model of congregational life and all theology of the congregation remain dead bones. Can these bones be made to live? (Ezek 37:1-14).

Come, Holy Spirit!

NAME INDEX

Abraham, 24
Amnesty International, 157, 166
Anderson-Larson, G., 102
Anselm of Canterbury, 77
Aquinas, T., 75
Augustine, 75

Barnabus, 77
Bellah, R., 18, 163
Berger, P., 133
Berry, W., xi
Bonhoeffer, D., 15, 72, 73, 75, 77, 84, 107, 133
Borg, M., 32
Bread for the World, 157, 166
Brueggemann, W., 46

Calvin, J., 77
Church World Service, 151
Clare of Assisi, 77
Congar, Y., 172
Constantine, 129

David, 116
Day, D., 75
Deborah, 24

Eck, D., 18, 115
Edwards, J., 77

Einstein, A., 41
Elijah, 77
Esther, 24, 77
Everist, N. C., 79
Ezra, 24

Fellowship of Reconciliation, 166
Folk, J., 160
Fowler, J. W., 73
Francis of Assisi, 77

Girard, R., 163, 164
Gregory of Nyssa, 77
Gutiérrez, G., 75

Habitat for Humanity, 151
Hall, D. J., 18, 20, 23
Hammarskjöld, D., 77
Hildegaard of Bingen, 75
Hippolytus, 11
Hirsch, S., 58
Hobbes, T., 132
Hommen, K., xi
Huffman, W., 62, 63

Ignatius, 2
Isaiah, 24
Ives, C., 77

Jeremiah, 77
Job, 90
Jordan, C., 77
Justin M., 11, 75

Karlstadt, A., 11
Kempe, M., 77
Kierkegaard, S., 75
King, M. L., Jr., 77
Kise, J. 58

Lee, A., 77
Locke, J., 132
Luther, M., 11, 33, 34, 35, 36, 42, 75, 79, 106,
    144

Macrina, 77
Mary Magdalene, 77
Mary, Mother of Jesus, 24, 116
Mayeroff, M., 104
McClendon, J. W., 77
Mead, L., 70, 71
Meals on Wheels, 162
Miriam, 24
Moses, 24, 116
Mother Theresa, 77

Paul, 3, 5, 33, 35, 36, 37, 38, 49, 87, 116, 122,
    129, 141, 143
Peck, M. S., 85

Peter, 129
Polycarp, 2
Pope John XXIII, 145
Prenter, R., 35

Rajashekar, P., 117
Rose of Lima, 77
Ruth, 77

Sample, T., 18, 20, 23
Sarah, 24
Schattauer, T., 62
Schwarz, C., 57, 58
Search Institute, 71
Sierra Club, 166
Smith, A., 100

Taylor, C., 19, 61
Theresa of Avila, 75
Tillich, P., 15
Truth, S., 77
Turner, V., 44

Vos, N., 79

Westerhoff, J., 57
World Council of Churches, 145, 146

Zwingli, 11, 34

SUBJECT INDEX

apocalyptic, 18, 20, 159, 160, 172
arcane discipline, 12, 70, 73, 80
Augsburg Confession, 34

baptism, 5, 6, 7, 34, 36, 37, 49, 69, 72, 87, 93,
  115, 128, 130, 131, 133, 134, 137, 141,
  143, 146, 152, 155, 172
basketball, 41
body of Christ, 19, 30, 47, 49, 50, 70, 87, 92,
  93, 131, 133, 134, 136, 142, 152

caring, 89, 95, 98, 104–7
catechism, 33, 74
Christendom/post-Christendom, xi, 25, 70, 71,
  73, 121, 129, 145, 152
civil religion, 18, 132, 133
community, 3, 4, 5, 6, 16, 17, 21, 24, 32, 38, 46,
  48, 58, 60, 73, 84f., 85, 87–89, 91–94, 98,
  105–8, 129, 131, 148, 150–52, 171
congregation, vii–ix, xii–xiii, 1, 7–12, 15–18,
  23–25, 29f., 49, 56–58, 63–66, 73, 78, 84,
  88, 90–95, 105, 107–8, 111–12, 115–23,
  128, 134–37, 146–52, 156–58, 161–62,
  164–67, 169–72
conventional wisdom, 32, 45, 51
countercultural, 3, 73
creation, 46, 61f., 64, 112, 160–61, 164
creed(s), 42, 46, 69, 127, 129, 134, 142, 170
cross, 5, 24, 31, 33, 36, 50, 64, 84, 86, 92, 104,
  114, 163, 164

culture, 18–23, 30, 43–44, 71, 84, 97, 99, 102,
  115–16, 121–23, 130, 135–37

diagrams, 9, 10
diakonia, 2, 5, 6
discipleship, 12, 70, 73, 76, 77, 107, 134

ecumenism, 50, 112, 144, 152
environment, 19, 21, 64, 107, 134, 145, 157, 161
epiclesis, 47, 169, 172
evangelizing, xiii, 51, 111–23, 171
Eucharist, 3, 12, 45–49, 51, 72, 87, 93, 141,
  149, 160, 163

faith, 2, 3, 5, 6, 11, 12, 17, 22, 30, 32, 33,
  35–38, 42, 48, 49, 52, 56, 57, 61, 65, 66,
  69, 70, 72–73, 75, 76, 77–78, 79f., 94, 115,
  118, 119–23, 128, 130, 131, 133, 136, 137,
  144, 170
family/family systems, 17, 21, 32, 49, 50, 66,
  86, 90, 105, 131, 156
forgiveness, 4, 5, 24, 25, 31, 33, 34, 36, 47, 48,
  51, 60, 75, 78, 85, 88, 90, 101, 105, 112,
  114, 144

God, vii, ix, xif., 1, 4, 7, 11, 15, 16–18, 23–26,
  29, 30–38, 42–52, 57f., 60–65, 75, 84, 87,
  89–92, 94f, 98–107, 111–14, 120, 121–23,
  133, 135, 150, 158, 160f, 164, 169, 172

gospel 3, 6, 7, 11, 17, 25, 30, 33–35, 38, 45, 46, 51, 63f., 85, 101, 112, 120, 128–34, 144, 172
grace, 4, 24, 30, 33, 36, 45, 51, 75, 85, 114, 144

healing, 5, 60, 67, 88, 91
Holy Spirit, 25, 30, 35, 42, 102, 114, 128, 149, 172
hunger, 47, 104, 107, 156f., 161–64

identity, xiif., 2, 6–9, 17, 25f., 45, 46, 49, 55–56, 73, 79, 93, 98, 107f., 111, 116, 130, 152, 169f.
idolatry, 98, 101–4, 120, 134
imagination, 41–45, 48, 77, 169

Jesus Christ, 2–5, 29f., 36, 38, 48, 56, 62, 69, 76, 85f., 101, 114, 121, 123, 128, 129, 130, 131, 133f., 145, 150, 152, 163
justice, 21, 24, 60, 64, 133, 156, 158–60, 164, 170
justification, 30, 36, 37, 38, 112, 143, 144, 170

keryama, 2–4, 6, 51
kingdom of God, 4, 29–33, 42–45, 46, 49, 51, 112, 134, 157, 160, 169
koinonia, 2, 4–6, 38

law, 37, 90, 98, 101, 103, 129, 132, 158f.
leader/leadership, viif., xii, 1, 8, 17, 23, 25, 58–59, 72, 87, 119, 121, 147, 151, 156, 164f., 170f.
liturgy, xii, 2, 8, 9–12, 44–45, 49, 50, 52, 75f, 80, 83, 87, 93, 97, 114, 134, 135, 160, 183
love, 4, 5, 15, 24, 33, 37, 38, 83f., 86f., 100, 103, 104, 113, 156

Myers-Briggs Type Indicator, 58–59
mission, vii–ix, xii, 2, 6, 7–9, 10, 18, 25, 29, 38, 49, 64, 65, 71, 80, 104, 107f., 111–12, 113–15, 121, 123, 128, 130f., 136f., 141, 144f., 152, 164, 165, 170
model, xii, 7–9, 23, 167, 169-172
money, 98, 102–4

nationalism, 128, 131f.

offering, 46, 49, 51, 97, 160, 165
ownership, 97, 98f.

parables, 29, 30f., 47, 61, 86, 156
paraenesis, 30, 36, 38, 49

pastor, 58–61, 63, 89–95, 119, 121, 122, 167
peace, 21, 24, 46f., 49, 64, 112, 128, 137, 156, 159, 163–64
persecution, 2, 71, 73, 129
poor, 19, 21, 47, 56, 62, 64, 100, 158f., 162f.
post-Christian, 19, 56, 70, 80, 116, 121, 123, 152, 172
prayer, xiii, 15, 32, 46f., 51, 57–67, 87f., 95, 107, 135, 141f., 150, 161, 172
pretending, 41, 45, 62f.
priesthood of all believers, 70, 79, 119, 172

race, 52, 87
reconciliation, 5, 34, 52, 60, 114, 142, 144, 149, 164
resurrection, 4, 24, 33f., 37, 114
ritual, xiii, 4, 34, 42–45, 51, 73, 83f., 132f., 149, 163

sacraments, 4, 34f., 48, 105, 141f.
saints, 47, 65, 76–80, 88, 107, 148
salvation, 28, 35, 60, 111f., 131, 152, 160
Scripture, 3, 10, 20, 33f., 46, 69, 74, 79, 144, 145
sin, 3, 4, 17, 24, 32f., 34, 35, 36, 37, 46, 75, 88f.
sinner, 114, 123, 144, 159
Small Catechism, 33
small groups, 56, 66, 87, 121f.
social ministry, 7, 51, 112, 155–67, 171
spiritual gifts, 15, 87
spirituality, 58f.
state, 18, 52, 70, 98, 131–34, 155, 158
stewardship, 56, 97–108, 122, 151f., 161, 162

testimony, 3, 4, 36, 77–79, 122, 141
tithing, 56, 98, 101–4

unconventional, 51, 134

violence, 19, 21, 24, 25, 106, 112, 135, 137, 163–64
visiting, 5, 16, 91

wealth, 5, 32, 50, 76, 87, 99, 100, 131
Word and Sacrament, 9–11, 29, 34, 35, 38, 45, 48, 76, 89, 107, 114, 119
workplace, 79, 105, 106
worship, vii, xii, xiii, 3, 7–12, 25, 34, 35, 38, 41–52, 61f., 63, 69, 78, 80, 93, 98, 101, 103, 105, 107, 121, 122, 127, 135, 148f., 169–71

youth, 72, 74, 9294, 136, 151

SCRIPTURE INDEX

HEBREW BIBLE

Exodus

2:23-25	158
3:7-9	158
22:21-24	158
22:25-27	158

Leviticus

| 25 | 158 |
| 25:8-24 | 158 |

Joshua

| 24:15 | 104 |

2 Samuel

| 8:15 | 158 |

1 Kings

| 10:9 | 158 |

Psalms

24:1	98
58	159
72	159
82	159

Isaiah

11:1-9	159
42:5-7	159
53:3	90

Jeremiah

| 22:13-16 | 159 |

Ezekiel

| 37:1-14 | 172 |

Micah

| 3:9-12 | 159 |

NEW TESTAMENT

Matthew

5:9	163
6:19-22	102
6:25-33	100
10:16	156
11:12	31
13:44	31
18:20	85
20:1-16	31
22:1-14	31
23:23	103
25:31-46	86, 100, 156
25:40	156
28:19-20	69, 123

Mark

1:44	117
4:3-9	31, 61
4:32	99
6:7-13	99
6:30-44	161
8:1-10	161
9:37	94
12:17	103

Luke

4:16-21	159
6:20-26	159
10:29-37	31, 61
11:1-4	67
11:20	31
12:15-21	159
12:33-34	159
15:1-2	159
15:11-32	31, 61
16:13	99, 159
16:19-31	159
16:31	156
17:20-21	31
18:1-8	31
18:22-25	159
19:45-46	159

John

13	83
16:12-15	83
17:20-21	141

Acts

2:6	128
2:42-47	159
2:44-45	4
4:32-37	99, 159
17:6	50

Romans

1–3	37
4–5	37

6	37
7	37
8	37
9–11	37
10:14-17	123
12–16	37

1 Corinthians

4:1	98
7:17-24	159
10:16-17	142
12	161
12:13	141
13:13	87

Galatians

2:19-20	75
3:28	87

Ephesians

4:5	128

Philippians

1:3-5	88

Colossians

1:20	164

1 Thessalonians

4:13-18	159

1 Peter

3:15	116

1 John

4:19	104

Revelation

7:9-10	131
22:12-21	159